Shaland's Lisbon

Shaland's Lisbon

An Illustrated Guide to Jewish History and Sites in and around Lisbon

Irene Shaland

GTA BOOKS

 GTA BOOKS

Shaland's Lisbon

Copyright © 2023 by Irene Shaland

All rights reserved. No part of this book may be reproduced in any form by any electronic or mechanical means including photocopying, recording, or information storage and retrieval without permission in writing from the author.

Cover by: Alex Shaland.

All photographs copyright © Alex Shaland unless otherwise credited. All rights reserved.

Paperback Edition ISBN: 979-8-9876115-0-0

Also by Irene Shaland

~ Jewish History and Travel ~
The Dao of Being Jewish and Other Stories
Shaland's Jewish Travel Guide to Malta and Corsica
~ Theater and Arts ~
Tennessee Williams on the Soviet Stage
American Theater and Drama Research 1945-Present

Dedication

To Alex, my love, always and forever. You are the reason and the inspiration for everything I do.

Table of Contents

Before You Go to Portugal	**1**
Brief Overview of the Sephardic History from Biblical Times to the Edicts of Expulsion	1
The Antiquity and the Roman Period	1
The Visigothic Period and the First Persecutions, 450-711	2
The Moors and the "Golden Age" of the Sefarad, 711-1492	3
The Beginning of the End, 1200s-1492	4
The Inquisition (1478) and the Edict of Expulsion (1492)	5
Why the Portuguese Story is Different: The Tale of Three Kings	6
The Great Sephardic Migration from Post-Expulsion Spain and Portugal	8
The Sephardic Diaspora as a New Phenomenon in History	10
LISBON	**12**
Planning Your Exploration of Lisbon	12
Starting Your Exploration of Lisbon	14
The Saint George Castle	14
Portuguese Reconquista and the Jews	16
The Jews during the first Portuguese kings	16
Looking for Lisbon Judiaries (Jewish Quarters): A Journey through Centuries	18
The Judiaria Grande (Great) or Judiaria Velha (the Old one)	18
The Judiaria Pedreira (Quarry)	22
Finding the Remaining Traces of Jewish Presence in Convento do Carmo	23
Judiaria Nova or Pequena (Small)	24
The Only Existing Former Jewish Quarter in Lisbon: Alfama	26

Understanding the Age of Discoveries (1400s-1600s) in Belém	33
The Belém Tower	33
The Beginnings of the Age of Discoveries	34
The Impact of the Jewish Scientists on the Age of Discoveries	39
Monument to the Discoveries in Belém	39
What exactly did the Jewish Scientists do?	41
Examples of the Manueline Style	45
Tombs of the Portuguese Greats in the Jerónimos Monastery	45
Belém Maritime Museum: Connecting with the Greatest Jewish Scientists of the Age of Discoveries	47
The Fundamental Works by Great Jewish Scientists that Made the Age of Discoveries Possible and Launched Modern Science	49
Key Achievements of the Sephardic Jewish Scientists in Portugal:	50
The Post-Conversion Jewish Story Continues: On the Trail of Massacres and Autos-da-Fé	51
The 1506 Massacre	51
Rossio Square or Praça Dom Pedro IV	54
The Most Beloved Public Show: the Auto-da-Fé	56
The Trail of the Inquisition in Lisbon	58
Why Almost No Traces of the Past Jewish Presence Can Be Found in Lisbon Today	60
The Infamous Earthquake of 1755 and Marquês de Pombal (1699-1782)	61
"Meeting" Marquês de Pombal in Lisbon	63
Lisbon Museums through the Lens of a Jewish History Explorer	65
The Rebirth of the Jewish Community in Lisbon	67
The Long Process of Judaism Legalization	67
Lisbon Shaare Tikvah Synagogue, 1904	68
Lisbon during World War II	71

Lisbon as a Nest of Spies and Josephine Baker (1906-1975)	72
Jewish Community of Lisbon during the Second World War and Today	75
The Jewish Museum is Coming to Lisbon!	77
SIDE TRIPS FROM LISBON	**79**
Sintra	79
Jewish Sintra	80
Pena Palace	81
National Palace	82
Cabo da Roca	85
Mafra	86
Mafra Library, priceless books, and the bats that "guard" them	88
The Hall of Portuguese Heroes and the Secrets of its Frescos	89
Who was this man we know as Christopher Columbus (1451-1506)?	93
Following the Steps of the Refugees from the Nazis during WWII	98
Ericeira	98
Cascais	100
Estoril	103
Ian Fleming, James Bond, spies, Estoril, and an unexpected Jewish connection	104
The Exiles Memorial Center and Museum or Espaço Memória dos Exílios	107
The Parting Words	109
About the Author	111

Acknowledgments

I owe a depth of gratitude to numerous entities and individuals that both inspired and enabled me to succeed in my quest to capture the Jewish narrative of Portugal.

First and foremost, I want to thank Mr. Michael Steinberger, Founder and CEO of the Jewish Heritage Alliance (JHA), an organization dedicated to introducing diverse audiences to the largely unknown Sephardic history. The JHA's brilliant programming, especially the lectures presented by Dr. Isaac Amon, Director of Academic Research and Program Development, was instrumental in sparking my interest in the story of Sefarad and strengthening my determination to delve deeper into that amazing history by traveling to Portugal to research and write this book.

Mr. Steinberger introduced me to Ruth Calvao, Member of the JHA Board, historian, and founder of Centro de Estudos Judaicos de Tras-os-Montes in Lisbon (Center for Jewish Studies in Tras-os-Montes, Iberian Historical and Cultural Routes). Ruth became my close friend, my mentor, and my Guru in all things Sephardic. In addition, she literally opened the doors for me to archival and museum collections. My new friend also curated my efforts to build a network of topic experts and Jewish leaders who would assist in my research.

My heartfelt thanks go to two key organizations within the Portuguese tourism industry that offered invaluable support: visitPortugal and the Center of Portugal Tourism.

Rita Febrer, Public Relations and Media Communications Manager at the New York Office of visitPortugal worked tirelessly to provide me with support in Lisbon and Porto. In addition, Rita's office treated me to the best Fado concert in Lisbon I have ever attended in either Portugal or the U.S.

My warmest thanks go to the managers and professionals from the Center of Portugal Tourism. Without their organizational support, my research of Portuguese history would not have reached the same depth as I was able to achieve. Marli Monteiro, Executive Director, and Antonio Belo, Head of the Center's Press, Trade, and Market Research, developed a detailed itinerary and provided highly knowledgeable professional guides, excellent accommodations at historic hotels, and typical meals at the best restaurants throughout the entire region of the center of Portugal.

My special thanks go to Mr. Isaac Assor, the founder and owner of Alegretur, the number-one travel agency in Portugal that specializes in historical tourism. A Rabbi and Jewish historian, Isaac advised me on my itineraries. His Alegretur agency organized most of my travel and provided excellent guides in Lisbon, Evora, Castello de Vida, and Porto.

Recommended by Isaac Assor, Antonio Barrosa, a Lisbon guide par excellence, was invaluable in deepening my understanding of the Jewish history of Lisbon. I am very grateful to Antonio for that remarkable tour, his suggestions, and additional images he provided for this book.

I extend my sincere thanks to the team of specialists at the Torre do Tombo (The National Archives of Portugal in Lisbon), who provided an unforgettable opportunity for me to visit this institution and witness the restoration and preservation of Inquisition records. I specifically want to mention Dr. Silvestre Lacerda, the General Director, who organized my visit; Anabella Ribeiro, the Manager; Jose Furtado, Public Relations and Information, who was my host and a guide there; and Sonia Domingos, the documents restorer, who patiently explained to me the contents of Inquisition records and showed how the manuscripts were restored and preserved.

I am very grateful to Andre de Quiroga, a journalist, politician, and historian of visual and culinary arts. During many Zoom sessions and our unforgettable dinner meeting in his house, Andre generously shared with me his multi-faceted expertise and knowledge of contemporary Portugal.

In our Zoom and phone conversations with Portuguese business and Jewish leaders Jose Bensaude Ulman Carp, Antonio Freire Bensaude, and Samuel Levy they shared priceless insight into the life of the modern Jewish community of Portugal and told me about the pioneering families that created it. And for that knowledge, I am eternally grateful.

I treasure our meetings, first virtually, and then in person in Paris, with Livia Parnes, a Jewish historian, and Jean-Jacques Salomon, a Vice-Chair of the Board of the future Jewish Museum in Lisbon, who shared with me exciting information about the status of this most important project.

Finally, I am deeply grateful to my dear friends, my daughter Michelle, and my husband Alex who selflessly dedicated their time to reading and re-reading my drafts of this book, applying their professional knowledge, excellent editorial aptitude, and superb sense of language to my every page. To my first readers, proofreaders, and editors – Sandra Kramer, Bob Berk, and Sophia Muchnik – I owe my gratitude.

Irene Shaland
November 2023. Cleveland Ohio.

Before You Go to Portugal

As the author of this Guide, I think that it is essential to understand the background of the Jewish story in Portugal before commencing the exploration on the ground, and therefore, I invite you to learn a few historical facts.

Brief Overview of the Sephardic History from Biblical Times to the Edicts of Expulsion

The Iberian or Sephardic (from Sefarad – Spain) Jewish narrative constitutes an integral part of not only overall Jewish but also world history, the course of which was radically changed by what some historians call, the Saga of Sefarad.

Whether you travel only to Lisbon and nearby towns or crisscross the entire country in pursuit of the Portuguese Jewish history, this Guide will assist you in learning about the greatest scientific and intellectual achievements of the Sephardic Jews. At the same time, you will learn about massacres, riots, expulsions, and forced conversions. During your journey, you will uncover little-known stories, one at a time, the historical trajectory of courage and strength, survival and rebirth.

The Antiquity and the Roman Period

Historians have difficulty determining when exactly the first Jews arrived in Iberia. Biblical scholars point out that in the Bible, there are mentions of the western Mediterranean known to ancient Israelites. For example, around 970 BCE, King Solomon had an alliance with the King of the Phoenicians, Hiram of Tyre, and provided him with Israelite sailors. Most probably, some of the Jewish tribes, like prosperous Asher, seafaring Zebulon, and the tribe of Dan (known for its judicial wisdom), sailed with the Phoenicians, helped to colonize the Mediterranean coast, and lived in the Phoenician territories. And, as some historians state, early Spanish Jewish documents refer to those tribes' descendants living in Iberia.

On Rosh Hashanah, we read from the Book of Jonah, who is commanded by his God to bring a message to the sinful people of Nineveh. That city was located in ancient Assyria, across the Tigris River from modern Mogul in Iraq. Jonah does not want to go there, and he runs away: he takes a ship going to the Phoenician-Jewish city Tarshish (Tartessus on the Guadalquivir River in southwestern Spain). That sounds like really good proof of Jews living in Iberia since Biblical times!

Jews definitely lived in Iberia during the Roman period, 218 BCE-19 CE. Josephus Flavius, a first-century CE Roman Jewish historian, mentions Jews moving from Judea to Sefarad or Hispania, which was the Roman name for the Iberian Peninsula.

The Visigothic Period and the First Persecutions, 450-711

The early Germanic people, the Visigoths, arrived in Iberia after the complete dissolution of the Roman Empire. The Visigothic Kingdom occupied what are now southwestern France and the Iberian Peninsula from the 5th century until the Moorish conquest in 711. That period was marked by the first series of anti-Jewish laws, such as the prohibition of intermarriages (in 305), expulsion and forced conversion (in 613), affirmation of the legality of forced baptism for the very first time in history (in 633), and prohibition of all Jewish customs and traditions, such as circumcisions, the celebration of holidays, and Kashrut, among numerous others (in 653). In addition, all Jews, even those who converted to Christianity, were prohibited from testifying in court.

As Benzion Netanyahu stated in his brilliant book *The Origins of the Inquisition*, (Random House, 1995), the middle of the seventh century was marked by, what he calls, the "racialization of religion." Jews began to be viewed not only as people of a religion different from Christianity, but also as a "race," biologically different from Christians, people of "pure blood."

The Moors and the "Golden Age" of the Sefarad, 711-1492

In 711, the Moors arrived from North Africa and conquered Iberia. They were the medieval Muslims, who established a great empire in the Iberian Peninsula. Called Al-Andalus, it extended from West Africa and Maghreb to what we know today as Portugal and Spain.

The Moors regarded Jews as People of the Book and treated them with tolerance and respect. Muslim rulers encouraged learning, science, and culture. Muslims, Christians, and Jews coexisted in a spirit of mutual tolerance. Jewish scholars from this period influenced European learning, and Al-Andalus became the "capital" of the world Judaism. In her book *The Ornament of the*

World, (Bay Back Books, 2003), Maria Rosa Menocal stated: "Tolerance was an inherent aspect of Andalusian society."

This period produced such great personalities in Jewish culture as: Hasdal Ibn Shaprut (915-975), a scholar, translator, and a powerful diplomat at the court of Abd Al-Rahman III; Solomon Ibn Gabirol (1021-1055), a poet and philosopher; Moses Ben Maimon or Maimonides (1138-1204), a medical doctor, philosopher, and the most influential Torah scholar in the Middle Ages, to name just a few.

The Beginning of the End, 1200s-1492

The 13th century started well for the Jews of Spain under Ferdinand III of Castile, Leon, and Galicia (1201-1252). He understood the value Jews brought to the kingdom, and his reign is regarded by historians as a turning point in the destinies of the Iberian Jews. He appointed a Jew, Don Meier, as the chief tax collector, as well as other Jewish high-level officials.

Despite the strong opposition of the Church, Ferdinand III confirmed a number of privileges for the Jews in several cities. For example, he allowed the Jews of Seville to retain their synagogue and also presented them with four small mosques to be transformed into synagogues. Ferdinand became the leader of the *Reconquista* (reconquest or liberation) movement liberating many cities in his country from the Moors. Wanting to be seen as a tolerant ruler, he called himself the "King of Three Religions."

The 14th century was marked by the Black Death, a plague that swept across Iberia and the rest of Europe (1348-1351), and that drastically changed the situation for the Jews. They were accused of poisoning wells and spreading the disease. Murderous pogroms followed from city to city and from country to country.

The worst massacre of the entire middle ages period happened in Seville in 1391. That was an unprecedented display of Jew-hatred and violence. Over 4,000 people were killed in a short span of time. The killing spread throughout the country, and overall, 50,000 to 100,000 Jews were viciously murdered in 70 towns in Spain within three months. Tens of thousands converted to Christianity.

It is estimated that by the 1400s, one third of the Jews in Spain were murdered, one third fled the country, and one third converted to Christianity, becoming the New Christians or *Conversos*, who turned into a new social group, despised, hated, and persecuted. The 15th century in Spain produced the "Blood Libel" with the case of the "Holy Child of Guarda" (1491) when Jews were accused of killing Christian children and using their blood to bake matzah.

The Inquisition (1478) and the Edict of Expulsion (1492)

In the 15th century, two events happened in Spain that forever changed the destiny and mentality of the Sephardic Jews and marked a cardinal turning point in world history.

In 1478, the Office of the Holy Inquisition was established with the feared Tomas de Torquemada (1420-1498) as the Great Inquisitor. He was obsessed with New Christians as secret Judaizers that had to be eradicated from the face of the Christian land. In 1492, the "Most Catholic Monarchs," King Ferdinand of Aragon and Queen Isabella of Castile, liberated Spain from the Moors and captured the last Moorish stronghold, Granada. The first matter of business for them was to turn their realm into a pure Catholic country. So, they issued the infamous "Alhambra Decree" or Edict of Expulsion, published in March of 1492: "We, with the counsel and advice of... great noblemen of our kingdoms... resolve to order the Jews and Jewesses of our kingdoms to depart and never to return..."

Many Jews fled to the Ottoman Empire, Greece, Turkey, North Africa, and across the border to Portugal. Estimates vary, but several sources state that more than 100,000 Jews arrived in Portugal after the Edict. According to historians, before the Alhambra Decree, Portugal had 32 Jewish communities. Following the Edict, Jewish refugees from Spain contributed to an unprecedented growth of communities numbering 139.

Why the Portuguese Story is Different: The Tale of Three Kings

King João II (1455-1495 ruled 1481-1495). He is known in Portuguese history as the first "modern" monarch, who worked to restore the status of the Portuguese Crown. According to some relatively recent and rather controversial accounts, it was King João II who sent a person, known to the world as Christopher Columbus, to the court of Ferdinand and Isabella of Spain, as a spy on a mission. According to some historians, the mission was to make the Spaniards believe that Columbus was going to discover for them the route to India but to give them instead the Caribbean islands. (More about that in this Guide's part devoted to Mafra.)

For the Jews, King João II was a benevolent ruler who, in 1490, directed city fathers of Lisbon to protect the

Jews from the frequent and violent anti-Jewish assaults. In 1492, he allowed more than 100,000 Jews to cross the border from Spain to Portugal. They all had to pay tax for the privilege, of course. However, later on, King João II became infamous for his persecution of the newly arrived Jewish refugees. He ordered the seizure of about two thousand Jewish children from their parents and converted them to Christianity. Then, ships took them to the island of São Tomé as settlers.

King Manuel I (1461-1521, ruled 1495-1521). Similarly to João II, his rule began with a reasonably benign attitude toward the Jews. He even released all the Jews who had been imprisoned during the time of King João II. However, when in 1496 he wanted to marry Infanta Isabella of Spain, daughter of the "most Catholic monarchs," Ferdinand and Isabella demanded that Manuel I got rid of the Jews who lived in his kingdom. So, in December 1496, Manuel I issued his Edict of Expulsion.

However, fearing the financial and economic collapse of his realm, he quickly changed his strategy from expulsion to forced conversion. The Jews of Portugal, including the former refugees from Spain, were tricked into believing that – if they did not wish to convert – they could come to Lisbon with their possessions and families, and the king's ships would be waiting in the port to take them out of the country.

Tens of thousands arrived, only to discover that there were no ships. These Jews were ambushed, robbed, beaten, and forcefully converted to Christianity, often just by sprinkling holy water on them. Some Jews preferred to kill their children and then themselves, but many chose life, even when that meant becoming what was called, the "New Christians." Shortly after, King Manuel I could report to his future in-laws, that there were no more Jews in his kingdom.

It is hard for us today to even imagine the magnitude of that tragedy. In the 15th century, the notion of a "secular Jew" did not exist. Deprived of their religion, traditions, books, and synagogues, the forcefully converted Jews felt lost and dead inside: people without identity, strangers to the world of the living. Unlike the situation in Spain after the Edict, the Portuguese Jews were forced to convert without the option of leaving the country. King Manuel I closed all borders, and they stayed closed for a while. To make things worse, the New Christians or *Conversos* became an obsession for the next king.

King João III (1502-1557, ruled 1521-1557). He was passionate about persecuting the *Conversos*. João III earned his infamous place in history as the king who brought the Inquisition to Portugal in 1536. The worst crime for the Inquisition was Judaizing or secretly observing Jewish traditions and rituals. So, the main target of the Holy Office of Inquisition became not the Jews – there were no Jews anymore in the entire Iberia – but the New Christians. Violent persecution of the New Christians continued for centuries. The Inquisition was abolished only in 1808 in Spain and in 1821 in Portugal.

The Great Sephardic Migration from Post-Expulsion Spain and Portugal

The following map illustrates the migration routes chosen by those Jews who decided and were able to leave their home countries, where they lived from the Biblical times.

The Jews fled to more hospitable lands such as those under the Ottomans, like Greece, Turkey, and North Africa.

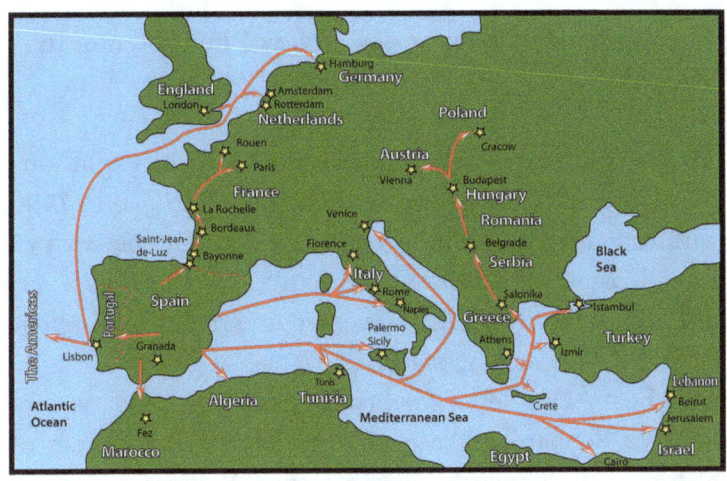

The Jewish migration after 1492-97.

The Portuguese Jews were also moving to Protestant countries and cities, such as Hamburg, Rotterdam, and Amsterdam, and to the Southwest of France, like Bordeaux and Bayonne. Many went to the New World, such as Brazil.

Map of Portugal.

The Sephardic Diaspora as a New Phenomenon in History

The establishment of the Inquisition and the expulsions, first from Spain in 1492 and then from Portugal in 1496, with the latter becoming almost immediately the edict of forced conversion, split all Sephardic Jews into two very different historic groups. We can name them "Those who left" and "Those who stayed."

"Those who left" formed a new phenomenon: the massive Sephardic Diaspora that altered the course of history. The Sephardic Jews of the Diaspora revitalized and recreated Jewish communities in Europe, formed new communities in the New World, and developed the "Jewish Atlantic" with trade routes that brought global trade to a previously unattainable level.

"Those who stayed" molded into a new social class, called either New Christians or *Conversos,* or in a derogatory way, *Marrano* (swine). Even generations after conversion, they still were considered *Marrano* and were despised and persecuted. As Alejandre Mendes stated in his 2008 book *Barros Basto, the Marrano Mirage*, (published in Portugal): "Marranos were not only exiles amongst the nations; they were exiles amongst the Jewish Nation."

After the initial forced conversions, for centuries, *Marranos* would be the subjects of suspicion, denunciations, arrests, torture, and burnings.

But the burnings of synagogues and Judaizers did not mean the end of Judaism. Judaism survived in secret rooms, cellars, and memories. And when Jewish books were forbidden and burned, People of the Book became People of the Memory. Despite the ruthless persecutions, Crypto-Judaism (beliefs of those who were forcibly converted to

Christianity but who secretly kept their ancestral faith alive) greatly influenced the world of the Sephardim for almost four hundred years.

Now, you are fully prepared for your explorations on the ground. With this Guide in hand, you will be visiting the sites to understand the lives of those who had no choice but to adapt to living in constant fear and yet kept their Jewish spirit alive.

Portugal and its capital city of Lisbon will gradually reveal their secrets to you, one site at a time.

And even if you do not plan to visit Portugal in the near future, reading this book will illuminate the history of the Jewish people in Portugal from prehistoric times through today.

LISBON

The Portuguese Jewish Narrative: Little-Known Stories That Changed the World

Planning Your Exploration of Lisbon

How to plan your time

Our recommendation is to spend two or three full days in Lisbon and dedicate two or three following days to day trips out of Lisbon to such fascinating places as Sintra, Cabo da Roca, Mafra, Ericeira, Cascais, and Estoril.

If you have a car, it is possible to combine Mafra and Ericeira with Cascais and Estoril into one long but exciting day. In this case, you can visit Sintra and Cabo da Roca on another day, therefore decreasing the number of side-trip days from three to two.

How to get around Lisbon

Portugal's charming capital city has great public transportation. Also, both Uber and taxis are very convenient and affordable. If you opt to buy a three-day Lisboa Card, your transportation in Lisbon and to Sintra, Cascais, and Estoril will be covered. In addition to transportation, the Lisboa Card covers some museums and offers discounts to many other places of interest. You can buy this card at the Tourist Information Office upon your arrival at the airport. You can pick up your city map there as well.

For the days you are in the city and the day in Sintra, the car is not needed. If you plan to travel throughout the country after Lisbon, we suggest to rent a car the day you go to Mafra. The most straightforward way is to get an Uber in the city, go to the airport and then rent your car there. If you need a car with automatic transmission, make sure you book your car months in advance.

Starting Your Exploration of Lisbon

We recommend to begin your exploration of Lisbon in the Saint George Castle.

The Saint George Castle

How to get to the castle

Either Uber or a taxi will be convenient. We preferred the free elevator rides that you can take from the Baixa neighborhood. But be warned: once you exit the elevator, you will have to walk a short distance uphill. While buying your entrance tickets for the castle, pick up the map and start wandering.

This castle towers over Lisbon and can be seen from almost anywhere in the city. The castle's oldest remaining

View of the Saint George Castle.

The Saint George Castle towers and walls.

part dates to the 6th century, or the end of the Roman period. The Romans called the entire land of modern Portugal the Province of Lusitania. Victorious Moors, who conquered the area in 714, used this castle as their royal residence.

The first Portuguese King Afonso Henriques (1109-1185), while leading the *Reconquista* (liberation or reconquering the country from the Moors), liberated the castle and the city of Lisbon in 1147 and made the castle his royal residence. English Crusaders, who were on the way to Jerusalem, helped King Afonso Henriques a great deal. Though the castle's dedication to the patron saint of England in gratitude for that help came much later, in the 14th century.

Afonso Henriques was called the "Conqueror." A widely-respected nobleman from the north of Portugal, he had a large army and conquered most of the land held by the Moors. In 1139, he was proclaimed King of Portugal,

Afonso the First. Afonso is credited with building one of Europe's first modern nation-states. So, you can look at the Castle of St. George as one of the key places where, arguably, the very first European nation-state was created!

Portuguese *Reconquista* and the Jews

By the time Afonso arrived in Lisbon, the Jews had been living there, most probably, since the Phoenician times when they arrived in their ships as sailors or colonizers. It would be fair to say that the Jewish population lived in the area of today's Portugal long before Portugal as a country was established.

Some archeologists believe that in the 4th century, the city was already surrounded by a wall. According to historians, when the Moors conquered Lisbon in 714, it became the largest city in their empire Al-Andalus. At that time, Lisbon's population reached around 20,000-25,000 inhabitants. Under Muslim benevolent rule, the population grew significantly, partly due to the influx of numerous Jewish merchants and money lenders.

The Jews during the first Portuguese kings

The *Reconquista* movement in Portugal began much earlier than in Spain. In the fight of Portuguese rulers against the Moors, the Jews who could speak Arabic served as envoys, interpreters, and spies.

After the reconquest of Lisbon by Afonso Henriques in 1147, the Jews were allowed to stay where they lived under the Moors: in the lower town and outside the city walls. Afonso, who valued the help provided by the Jews, granted a Jewish man named Yahia Ben Yahi the post of the Royal

Tax Collector. Soon, the king appointed Ben Yahi as the first Chief Rabbi of Portugal. Afonso understood that Jews were important for the economy of his kingdom.

In 1170, the king granted charters to the non-Christian merchants living in Lisbon, including the Jews. These charters gave the Jewish population freedom of worship and made them subjects of Portuguese law. The next king, Sancho I (1154-1211, ruled 1185-1211) continued his father's policies toward the Jews.

In 1189, he protected the Jews of Lisbon from violent Crusaders, and even forcibly removed those rioting knights from the city. Sancho I appointed a Jew, Jose Ibn-Yahya to serve as High Steward of the Realm.

Afonso Henriques, the Conqueror. This monument is located in the city of Afonso's birth, Guimarães.

Due to its strategic location, Lisbon became the capital of Portugal in 1255.

Jews held important political and economic posts until the late 15th century. One such person was Don Isaac Abravanel (1437-1508), the greatest Jewish personality before the Expulsion of the Jews from Portugal in 1496, who served as a treasurer at the court of Alfonso V.

Looking for Lisbon Judiaries (Jewish Quarters): A Journey through Centuries

Some of the content in our *Judiaries* section is based on the data from the website put together by Questom Judaica, a consortium of Portuguese historians: https://questomjudaica.blogspot.com/2013/11/lisboa.html

For a deep dive into Lisbon's Jewish history, we will reconstruct the past while traveling not only through the modern city but also through time. To find *Judiaries*, we advise you to use a GPS app on your smart phone to guide you to the streets and the landmarks we point out. To help you plan an itinerary that best suits your location and the time you have, mark those places on the city map as well. We also ask you to "pack" your patience and your imagination. Think of your exploration as mental archeology.

The Judiaria Grande (Great) or Judiaria Velha (Old)

Below are the photos of the current names of some streets that were bordering Judiaria Grande.

Street signs, Judiaria Grande. All three images are courtesy of Antonio Barrosa.

Find the **Church of Our Lady of [Immaculate] Conception (Igreja de Nossa Senhora da Conceição Velha)** on the street Rua da Alfândega 108.

Rua da Conceição or Conception that leads to Igreja de Nossa Senhora da Conceição Velha.

The Great Synagogue of Lisbon, built in 1307, was most probably located where this church currently stands. The synagogue was destroyed after 1497, when King Manuel I changed the Edict of Expulsion of the Jews from Portugal issued in 1496 to the Edict of the Forced Conversion. A church was built on the spot where the synagogue used to stand.

That church was later destroyed by the great earthquake of 1755 that leveled almost the entire capital. The beautiful Manueline-style church that you see today was constructed after the earthquake.

The Judiaria Grande was the most important and most populated Jewish neighborhood in medieval Lisbon. The neighborhood originated in the place that was

Igreja de Nossa Senhora da Conceição Velha. Courtesy of Antonio Barrosa.

designated during the Moorish rule as the "Jewish area." Its approximate location is most likely somewhere between **the churches of Santa Madalena** and **São Nicolau.**

Most professionals of the Jewish community lived there. That Judiaria Grande was also the place where the **Jewish City Council** assembled. It was probably located near **Rua dos Mercadores, Rua de São Nicolau**, and **Rua da Conceição.**

Close to the Great Synagogue, stood the most important public buildings, such as the three hospitals: one – for the poor, another – for the community, and the third one was a men's hospital. There was also a center for the study of various sciences, including astronomy, cartography, geography, medicine, and mathematics. Among other buildings, there was a school, a bookstore, a bathhouse, and a butchery. An inn and a jail were built in the same area.

The streets were named after the professions of the people who lived and worked there, like merchants, textile dyers, and silk fabric makers, to name just a few. This area was the heart of Jewish life in Lisbon, and most of these facilities were used by the entire Jewish community of the city.

Historians estimate that, at that time, the Jews of Lisbon constituted over 10 percent of the city's population. The Jewish traders of Lisbon from Judiaria Grande had connections with their co-religionists throughout Europe, North Africa, and the Near East. Medical doctors, lawyers, philosophers, cartographers, mathematicians, and other professionals lived in that Judiaria as well. All those people made Grand Judiaria essential to the vitality of Lisbon's economy.

This was most probably the neighborhood where the great **Isaac Abravanel** lived and where the world-famous Lisbon Bible was created. The Lisbon Bible is considered by specialists as one of the very best codexes of medieval Hebrew illumination. (A codex is a manuscript produced in the form of a book rather than as a scroll). This Bible is used in modern critical editions as a model text because it is believed to be one of the most beautiful and precise Hebrew biblical manuscripts. Completed in 1482, the Lisbon Bible is the witness to the rich cultural life of the Portuguese Jews before the expulsion and forced conversion of 1496-97. You can see this Bible in the British Museum of London (now called the British Library) that bought it in 1882.

The Judiaria Pedreira (Quarry)

This Judiaria was located near today's **Largo do Carmo** in the trendy Chiado neighborhood. You can walk there easily from Rossio Station.
The synagogue that used to stand there was built in 1260, almost 50 years before the Great Synagogue of Lisbon.

Right: Largo do Carmo.

The Jews of this Judiaria were pushed out by King Dinis during 1317-19. Why? That was not an expulsion. The king just wanted to give a couple of presents to his favorite, Admiral of Portugal, Manuel Pessanha. And those presents were the synagogue building and the surrounding area. This area was entirely ruined by the earthquake of 1755.

Largo do Carmo is a charming square with an elaborate fountain and Brazilian Jacaranda trees. A memorial located on the square commemorates the April 1974 Carnation Revolution: an armored personnel vehicle reminds us of the peaceful end of Antonio Salazar's totalitarian regime.

Armored personnel vehicle on Largo do Carmo.

Finding the Remaining Traces of Jewish Presence in Convento do Carmo

Just a few minutes' walk from the Largo do Carmo brings you to the strangely beautiful and romantic ruins of **Convent do Carmo**. After the 1755 earthquake destroyed the convent, Marquês de Pombal, who led the rebuilding of the capital city, wanted the elegant arches from the 12th century to be left

Ruins of Convent do Carmo. Now, Museum of Archeology.

standing as they were, with an open sky instead of the roof.

The structure serves as a poignant reminder of the catastrophic earthquake. This ancient convent is a branch of the National Museum of Archeology (Museu Nacional de Arqueologia), and there you find a collection of tombstones with Hebrew inscriptions.

Tombstones with Hebrew inscriptions.

Judiaria Nova or Pequena (Small)

When the Jews were evicted from Judiaria Pedreira in 1317-19, they settled in a very small area – Judiaria Nova or Judiaria Pequena. That was indeed a *pequena* (small) Jewish Quarter consisting of only one street called back then **Rua da Judiaria.** We were told that today we can trace it mentally from the front of the Bank of Portugal on Rua Aurea to the doors of the church of São Julião.

Below are a few views of the Small Judiaria.

Streets in what used to be the Small Judiaria. Photo courtesy of Antonio Barrosa.

Streets in what used to be the Small Judiaria. Photo courtesy of Antonio Barrosa.

Square in what used to be the Small Judiaria. Photo courtesy of Antonio Barrosa.

The Only Existing Former Jewish Quarter in Lisbon: Alfama

The word *alfama* means fountains in Arabic.

Fountains in Alfama.

Since Alfama was not destroyed by the catastrophic earthquake in 1755, it exists as the oldest neighborhood in Lisbon, located on the hills between St. George Castle and the Tagus River. Despite its Arabic name, Alfama is considered to date back to the Visigothic period between the 6th and the 8th centuries.
During the Moorish rule, Alfama became a bustling neighborhood. Fishermen and sailors lived there for centuries.

The Royal shield decorates the fountains: a reminder that Alfama exists only due to Royal kindness.

Find your way to a small square called **Largo de São Miguel**. A small street leading to the square, **Beco de São Miguel**, is one of the oldest streets in Lisbon. It was not destroyed by the earthquake.
The pink house at number 15 on Beco São Miguel facing the square is considered the oldest house in Lisbon.

Street sign on Beco de São Miguel.

Right: Number 15 on Beco São Miguel, the oldest house in Lisbon.

Across the square from number 15 on Beco São Miguel is the site, which was originally selected for the future Daniel Libeskind's Jewish Museum of Portugal.

Original site for the Jewish Museum on Largo de São Migueel.

Some of Alfama streets are so narrow, that I remembered the line from the beloved Portuguese Renaissance poet Luís de Camões: "Our lips meet easily, high across the narrow street."

Largo de São Rafael.

Walking narrow streets of Alfama.

Rua do Espirito Santo, Alfama.

Alfama **Jewish Quarter** dates to the middle of the 1300s. It became a ghetto when the first segregationally-focused law in the mid-1300s required that the Jews be locked from the outside after the church bells called for evening prayers. King Pedro I (1320-1367, ruled 1357-1367), who passed that law, was very strict about the movement of the Jews outside their community at night.

Rua da Judiaria reminds us that there was once a bustling Jewish neighborhood. Strolling along the ancient streets you might notice a few traces of the former Jewish quarter.

Street sign.

The Alfama **synagogue** was built in 1373-1374 near the **Torre de São Pedro**, close to the church of the same saint.

Left: Torre de São Pedro on Rua de São da João da Praça.

It consisted of four big two-story rooms and a balcony overlooking the alley. Since the Jews built their synagogue without royal consent, they were forced to pay a penalty of 50 pounds of gold.

Right: The likely location of the Alfama synagogue.

Ground level of the possible Alfama synagogue.

The second floor of the possible synagogue.

Left: The possible location of the Rabbi's house next to the synagogue.

Understanding the Age of Discoveries (1400s-1600s) in Belém

Continue your immersion into Portuguese history and your journey through centuries. You will now be entering the Age of Discoveries. This era encompasses the most remarkable period not only in the history of Portugal but also in the history of Europe. To understand that, you need to travel to the western district of Lisbon, **Belém**.

How to get to Belém
You can get to Belém by train, cab, or Uber. If you have the Lisboa Card, it covers the train line going from the station called Cais do Sodre in Lisbon. The train ride will take less than 10 minutes.

In Belém, the Age of Discoveries, that made Portugal the wealthiest country in Europe, is celebrated, flamboyantly and in stone.

The Belém Tower

The **Belém Tower** (also called the Tower of Saint Vincent) was built in 1515-1520 and is located in Jardim da Torre de Belém. Most voyages in the Age of Discoveries departed from here. And it was this tower that welcomed sailors' safe return back home.

It is widely accepted that the Portuguese were the founders of nautical science. Before the Age of Discoveries, maritime explorations had been largely conducted by small private companies or by adventurous captains. But never by the state government.

Each new generation was almost as oblivious to the findings of those daring explorers as the generations before them. Why?

Right:
The Belém Tower.

The answer is simple: no record keeping. Few of those captains bothered to record any details of their adventures, keep logs, or create charts. Without detailed documentation of accumulated experience, their voyages had little value. The navigational style during the middle ages is often described as "by God and by guess." In addition, most of these expeditions were focused on the Mediterranean Sea only. The Atlantic Ocean was thought of as the Ocean of Darkness or the Boiling Sea. And then, the Portuguese changed everything.

The Beginnings of the Age of Discoveries

Most historians consider **Henry the Navigator** (1394 Porto - 1460 Sagres) the most important historical personality that ushered in the Age of Discoveries. However, some researchers trace the beginning of Portugal's pioneering role in maritime explorations back to the 13th century. In 1279, King Dinis (1261-1325, ruled 1279-1325) envisioned his country's future with ocean-going ships discovering unknown lands and decided to upgrade the Portuguese Navy.

The king hired a captain from Genoa and put him in charge of this project. He also ordered the planting of trees along the Portuguese Atlantic coast to provide timber for shipbuilding. Soon, Portuguese captains became the best in Europe.

They sailed the most maneuverable kind of ship, the groundbreaking Portuguese invention: the caravel.

Right: Model of a caravel.

The first caravels were probably built in the 13th-century Portugal and were used for off-shore fishing. In the mid-14th and then in the 15th century, these small and highly-maneuverable ships were upgraded to enable explorations along the West coast of Africa and further away, into the Atlantic Ocean. In addition to their small size, Portuguese caravels had a new invention – the lateen sail. Triangular in shape, the sails were mounted at an angle on the mast. This revolutionary design gave caravels superior speed and the ability to sail windward.

In the 1340s, three Portuguese caravels sailed from Lisbon to discover and then explore the Canary Islands, located near the northwestern coast of Africa.

Spain later seized those islands, but nevertheless, that was the first official maritime exploration done by a European state and not by individuals. The discoveries of the Canary Islands in the 1340s and of the Azores and Madeira archipelagos in the 1430s were the first two major breakthrough European explorations outside the Mediterranean.

In addition to the Royal patronage, overall meticulous planning, and the fantastic little caravels, the Portuguese, unlike any other nation at the time, were continuously and methodically applying the latest innovations in the fields of navigation and cartography to solving the challenges raised by the long voyages.

Infante Henrique or **Prince Henry the Navigator**.

He became, arguably, the greatest individual who raised the Portuguese maritime explorations to the highest level, unattainable by any other nation during his time. Henry was born in 1394 in Porto as a middle son of King João I and his Queen, Philippa Lancaster of England (as a side note for you, Shakespeare aficionados, she was a sister of Henry IV of England).

In Lisbon, you can "meet" Prince Henry's father on Praça da Figueira – one of the majestic squares rebuilt after the earthquake of 1755. (You will read more about Henry's parents in our upcoming Guide to Central Portugal and its chapter on Batalha).

Henry had his own plans for his mission in life: unlike his brothers and nephews, he was not interested in becoming a king. Henry grew up a religious man and

Praça da Figueira (Fig Tree Square). The statue of King João I (1357-1433) is in the center.

became a Grandmaster of the powerful and wealthy Order of Christ. (You will read more about this soldier-monks brotherhood in our upcoming Guide to Central Portugal and its Tomar chapter.)

Henry was a genius scholar and a brilliant visionary, far ahead of his time. At the same time, he was a very talented program manager, if we use modern terminology. And as such, it was Henry who became the brains behind the Portuguese most courageous and enterprising sea voyages. Henry understood the crucial role of sciences and founded the Academy of Nautical Sciences in Sagres, located at what was considered in Portugal, the end of the known world. As the Portuguese much-loved poet Luís de Camões said: "Where the land ends and the sea begins." See the map on the following page.

Madeira (1420) and Azores (1427) were discovered during voyages originating from Sagres. And it was in his beloved Sagres that Henry died in 1460. He died before the Golden Age of Portugal, before Bartolomeo Dias navigated around the Cape of Good Hope and Vasco de Gama discovered the sea route to India. The map below shows the key Portuguese explorations during the Age of Discoveries.

Right: Map of Portugal. Sagres is in the bottom-left corner of the country.

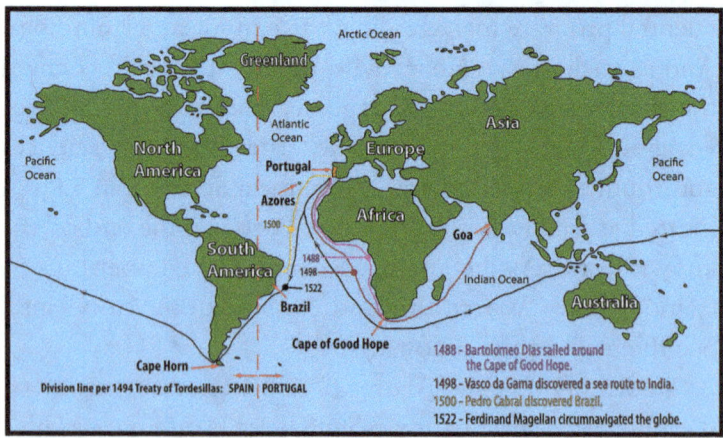

Portuguese explorations in the 15th and 16th centuries.

The Impact of the Jewish Scientists on the Age of Discoveries

Can we call Henry the first in the world pioneer of inclusivity? He recruited the very best, the most innovative and brilliant minds that existed in his time. And he did not care if they were Christians, Muslims, or Jews. Thanks to Henry, who was never concerned with a person's religion, during this period, Sephardic Jewish scientists played a highly important role in changing the map of the known world. Their scientific inventions and mathematical charts were fundamental in turning a small country like Portugal into the leader of European knowledge.

And to "meet" these scientists, you have to go to Belém.

Monument to the Discoveries in Belém

First, go to the east side of this 1960s monument to meet the key players of the era.

Note that the monument is shaped like a caravel. Of course, Henry the Navigator is in the front. He holds a model of the caravel and a map. Behind him, holding a sword is Vasco da Gama. Magellan, who circumnavigated the globe, holds a circle that represents the round Earth.

But it is on the west side of the monument that you find some of the greatest Jewish scientists.

To begin, notice the first two easily recognizable figures. The great Portuguese soldier-poet **Luís de Camões** holds his famous poem *The Lusiads* written on a scroll. The only

Monument to the Discoveries, east side.

Monument to the Discoveries, west side.

woman is **Philippa of Lancaster**, Henry's mother. Now, look for three specific figures behind Henry. As pointed out by a website madaboutlisbon.com, count from the front, when Henry is number 1: **Pedro Nunes** will be number 6,

Jácome de Maiorca is number 8, and **Pêro da Covilhã** is number 9. Please note, that this website does not identify the above-mentioned scientists as being Jewish.

What exactly did the Jewish Scientists do?

The voyages of discovery could succeed only when the groundbreaking scientific theories and newly developed navigational instruments were used to solve the navigational problems. Henry the Navigator and, after his death, the royal house of Portugal generously supported visionary scientists and their forward-looking scientific research in multiple disciplines. That was not science for the sake of science.

What the kings of Portugal wanted most of all was to ensure Portuguese naval supremacy and to achieve competitive advantage over other nations in trade. And while at it, build up enormous wealth. Among the leaders in the Portuguese scientific ventures were Jewish scholars or those of Jewish origin.

Jácome de Maiorca (lived possibly during the late 1300s-early 1400s)

Maiorca was a lead cartographer in the employ of Henry the Navigator. He was a genius of cartography who added newly discovered territories and trade routes to the quickly changing map of the world. Maiorca's techniques were an integral part of Sagres teachings. As mentioned above, Jácome de Maiorca's figure is found on the west side of the Monument to Discoveries.

Yehuda Ibn Verga (lived during the second half of the 15th century)

Yehuda Verga was born in Seville, Spain. After immigrating to Portugal, Verga became known as a genius mathematician, astronomer, historian, and kabbalist. Among his many groundbreaking works were: *Kizzur ha-Mispar* (a book on arithmetic), *Keli ha-Ofeki* (a manual for his astronomical instrument, which was used to find the sun's meridian), and a manual explaining how to determine the height of the Sun in the sky, just to name a few.

Abraham or Abraao Zacuto (1452-1515)

One of the greatest among the great, Abraham Zacuto held a position of Royal Astronomer at the court of King João II. In addition, he was a rabbi, historian, astronomer, and mathematician. Zacuto was born in Salamanca, Spain. He came to Lisbon in 1492 after the Edict of Expulsion from Spain. Zacuto's astrolabe and his navigational charts and tables allowed Portugal to achieve its exploration successes. Vasco da Gama and Christopher Columbus used Zacuto's navigational charts and instruments. In our time, one of the Moon craters, crater Zagut, was named after him.

Pedro Nunes (1502-1578)

Pedro Nunes was born to a *Converso* family. He is one of the most prominent mathematicians of his time renowned for his fundamental contribution to the nautical sciences. Pedro Nunes was the first to apply mathematics to navigation and cartography. He proposed the idea of a loxodrome (arc crossing all meridians of longitude at the same angle). Nunes also invented several measuring instruments that became essential for maritime explorations. Nunes is depicted on the west side of the Monument to Discoveries.

Pêro da Covilhã (circa 1460-circa 1526)

A *Converso*, Pêro da Covilhã was not a scientist but instead became a renowned Portuguese diplomat and explorer. He first rose to work for King Afonso V as a squire, and then in 1487, during the rule of King João II, he became an explorer of new lands and a spy for the king. Pêro da Covilhã's overland expeditions led him to India, before the sea route was officially announced by Portugal as one of their many discoveries. He explored trade opportunities with the Indians and Arabs. Da Covilhã also reached northeastern Africa and Ethiopia. His detailed reports were eagerly read in Lisbon. In many respects, it was thanks to da Covilhã, that Portugal became the world's leading center of knowledge concerning global geography and trade routes. Pêro da Covilhã is also depicted on the Monument to Discoveries.

We suggest that your next exploration point in Belém should be the **Jerónimos Monastery**.

Admire the immensity of this picturesque architectural masterpiece. Built with white limestone, the monastery and its church extend 900 feet along the waterfront. King Manuel I envisioned this Gothic structure adorned with Manueline-style ornamentation as his gratitude to God

Jerónimos Monastery.

Before sailors embarked on their journey, they stayed and prayed in Jerónimos Monastery.

Cloister, Jerónimos Monastery.

for all the discoveries made by the Portuguese explorers. It took more than 100 years to build the monastery.

Examples of the Manueline Style

Both the Belém Tower and the Jerónimos Monastery are some of the best examples of the Manueline-style buildings in Portugal. **The Manueline style** was not an architectural style. It was purely decorative. The Manueline style was developed during the reign of King Manuel I to demonstrate to the world the glory of Portugal. Look at the decorative elements. They all reflect maritime voyages: ship ropes, exotic fruits like artichokes, and faces of natives from faraway lands. You will find elements of the Manueline style in buildings of that period everywhere throughout Portugal.

Column with sculpted faces of exotic people. Inside the Church of the Jerónimos Monastery.

Tombs of the Portuguese Greats in the Jerónimos Monastery

Vasco da Gama is celebrated through the centuries for his expedition to India by way of the Cape of Good Hope (1497-1499). He was the first navigator who was able to sail from Europe to Asia, finding the way from the

Atlantic to the Indian Ocean. Portugal was able to build a great empire stretching from Europe to Africa and Asia largely because Vasco da Gama discovered the sea route to India.

The tomb of Vasco da Gama (1460-1524). The first explorer who sailed from Europe to Asia.

Luís de Camões was a Portuguese Renaissance writer and a military hero. In addition to being an adventurer and a soldier, Luís de Camões was a talented poet, who is considered a Portuguese Homer. He glorified his country as a great nation of maritime explorers. It was Luís de Camões who forever named his homeland the place "where the land ends and the sea begins." This apt description is quoted in most books about Portugal. He is also famous for his great poem *The Lusiads*. It was written in 1572 and dedicated to Vasco da Gama.

The tomb of Luís de Camões (1524-1580).

Belém Maritime Museum: Connecting with the Greatest Jewish Scientists of the Age of Discoveries

The place to see the inventions of the great Jewish scientists is Belém Maritime Museum. Once you enter the museum, look for the navigational instruments that made the Portuguese maritime explorations possible. These instruments enabled Portugal to obtain great wealth and power.

Some of those instruments were improved versions of the ancient designs, some were new inventions. And many of them were developed by Jewish scientists or scientists of Jewish origin.

Among those instruments are:

The astrolabe is an ancient astronomical instrument that allows the user to precisely calculate the position of celestial bodies.

The armillary sphere is a model representing celestial objects built as a group of rings with either Earth or the Sun at the center. The rings represent lines of celestial longitude and latitude. King Manuel I chose this sphere as his emblem.

Right: The display of instruments, many of which were developed by scientists of Jewish origin.

The astrolabe.

The armillary sphere.

The Fundamental Works by Great Jewish Scientists that Made the Age of Discoveries Possible and Launched Modern Science

As Baruch Spinoza said: "So long a man imagines that he cannot do this or that, so long it is impossible to him." Indeed.

At the Évora Public Library Archives, we had a unique opportunity to see ancient books that made the Age of Discoveries possible. Accompanied by Sofia Vieira, a specialist in Jewish history and Sephardic cuisine, we were allowed to view and photograph such rare books as Abraham Zacuto's *Almanach Perpetuum* and Francisco Faleiro's *Guias Nauticos de Évora* (Treatise on the Sphere and

Top: Abraham Zacuto's *Almanach Perpetuum*.
Right: The author, right, and Sofia Vieira study ancient books.

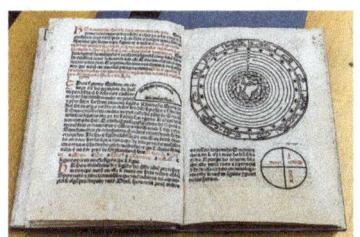

Francisco Faleiro's *Guias Nauticos de Évora* (Treatise on the Sphere and on the Art of Navigation.)

on the Art of Navigation). You are already familiar with Abraham Zacuto. Francisco Faleiro was a 15th-century Jewish astronomer and mathematician from Covilhá.

Key Achievements of the Sephardic Jewish Scientists in Portugal:

- **Made** major contributions to mathematics, astronomy, cartography, medicine, philosophy, economics, and other scientific areas

- **Enabled** the use of science and technology for solving navigational problems

- **Ensured** Portuguese naval supremacy

- **Established** a foundation for modern science in general and nautical science in particular

The Post-Conversion Jewish Story Continues: On the Trail of Massacres and *Autos-da-Fé*

As we mentioned previously, after 1497, the Sephardic Jewish narrative splits into two distinctly different directions: history of those who managed to leave the country and history of those who had to convert and stay. While you are still in Lisbon, make it a point to follow the steps of the Jews who became *Conversos* and stayed there.

The 1506 Massacre

In the city center, find a small square called **Largo de São Domingos**. The **Lisbon massacre** (sometimes called the **1506 Easter Slaughter**) started there in April 1506. During Easter of that year, a large crowd of local Christians and foreign sailors, inspired by the Dominicans and by their own deep-seated hatred of the Jews, pursued, tortured, murdered, and burned at the stake many thousands of New Christians.

This slaughter took place during the reign of King Manuel I, nine years after the expulsion and forced conversions and thirty years before the Inquisition was established in Portugal. Legally, there were no Jews at that time, not only in Lisbon but in the whole country of Portugal. That "minor" detail did not matter.

Look at the church **Igreja de São Domingos de Lisboa** located in the center of this square.

It was here that the massacre began on Sunday, April 19, 1506. People gathered in the church for a Sunday service. They were asking God to end the drought and the plague.

Right: The Church of São Domingos.

Then, someone saw light illuminating the face of Jesus. Was it a message from God, a miracle? But one of the New Christians, a skeptical Jew as he was, voiced his opinion: no, it was not a miracle, but rather light coming from a candle. He was grabbed by his hair and dragged outside. Then, the crowd beat him to death and burned his body in Rossio Square.

The crowd did not stop with a single Jewish corpse. For many, the great Easter entertainment was just beginning. Any person identified as a New Christian on the streets, man, woman, or child, became scapegoat to pay for the death of Christ, the drought, the plague, or just an object of violent fun.

Dominicans were giving absolution to murderers of the "heretics." What an inspiration! So, a happy crowd chased and killed anybody who they thought was a New Christian. They even dragged their victims out of their homes. The bodies were burned in Rossio Square or near the Tagus River.

The killing and the burning of dead or alive Jews in Rossio Square was going on for three days, when more and more locals joined in. The blood-thirsty crowd did not spare even Jewish infants tearing them apart or smashing their heads against the wall. They also looted the homes of New Christians grabbing gold, silver, and whatever else they could find. Thousands of Jews were murdered.

A recent monument on the square commemorates this horrible event. The sign says: "In memory of the thousands of Jews who were victimized by intolerance and religious fanaticism, killed in the massacre that started on 19 April 1506, on this square."

A short quote from the Book of Job is engraved on the base: "O earth, cover not thou my blood, and let my cry have no place."

Monument on Largo de São Domingos.

Right: The memorial in front of the Church of São Domingos.

Directly in front of the entrance to the church, there is a memorial dated September 26, 2000. The plaque on the memorial contains the text written by the Patriarch of Lisbon where he condemns the genocide of the Jews and expresses his regrets for the lives lost.

After only two minutes walking from the Largo de São Domingos you will find yourself in the beautiful Rossio Square.

Rossio Square or Praça Dom Pedro IV

Due to the elongated shape of the square, historians speculate that during the Roman period some 2,000 years ago, there was probably a racetrack. We could not help but admire the elegant classicism of this square today with its graceful column, fountain, and the building of the National Theater. Beautiful, typically Portuguese, pavement is a stone mosaic resembling waves of the sea. Atop the column stands a statue of Pedro IV, King of Portugal and Emperor of Brazil (1798-1834). Nothing will tell you about the burnings of the Jews that took place there in 1506.

Come closer to the National Theater to admire its perfect classical architecture. The National Theater was built on the place of the Inquisition Headquarters and the prison, both destroyed by the earthquake.

Rossio Square, the sight of burnings during the 1506 massacre.

The National Theater.

The Most Beloved Public Show: the *Auto-da-Fé*

"It's a lovely day for drinking and for watching people fry." From the song *Auto-da-Fé* in Leonard Bernstein's musical (1956) based on Voltaire's *Candide*.

After visiting the small Largo de São Domingos and the elegant Rossio Square, wander south towards the river Tagus. You will arrive at the largest and most magnificent square in Lisbon, the **Commerce Square or Praça do Comércio**.

The Commerce Square or Praça do Comércio.

Prior to the 1755 earthquake, this square was called Terreiro do Paço (the Palace Square). Since the days of Afonso I, the kings of Portugal resided in the St. George Castle. Then, King Manuel I decided to build a new palace in the center of the city, near the water. It was named the Ribeira Palace. The Ribeira Palace complex was redesigned and reconstructed a number of times from the original

Manueline-style design. That Baroque palace was destroyed in the 1755 earthquake along with most of Lisbon. After the earthquake, King José I (1714-1777, ruled 1750-1777) moved his residence to a nearby suburb of Ajuda. The Ribeira Palace was never rebuilt. But even today, people often refer to Lisbon's Commerce Square as the Palace Square.

If you plan to visit the **National Tiles Museum** in Lisbon, located approximately 3 km east of Praça do Comércio, make it a point to find a jaw-dropping panorama of Lisbon before the earthquake made of Azulejo tiles. In the center of the panorama you will see the Palace Square. (Read more in our part dedicated to Lisbon Museums from the Jewish perspective).

And it was there, on the **Palace Square**, where *autos-da-fé* took place in Lisbon. The very first one was on the 20th of September 1540. More *autos-da-fé* followed, with the last one taking place in 1761. The term *auto-da-fé* means "the act of faith" in both Spanish and Portuguese.

Defined by dictionaries as "public ceremonies," this was when the sentences of the accused were read for all to hear. Then, the criminals or rather "heretics" were ceremonially delivered to civic authorities who executed the punishments. "Judaizing" or secretly following the Jewish faith was deemed by the Inquisition as the worst crime imaginable. The sentencing and "relaxing" (or burning alive) of the heretics were staged as a grand-scale spectacle. People came from as far away as 50 kilometers to watch and be entertained.

After visiting the three squares in central Lisbon, you would have already walked part of the "Trail of the Inquisition."

The Trail of the Inquisition in Lisbon

Visiting the National Archives of Portugal (**Arquivo Nacional da Torre do Tombo**), and its collection of the Inquisition documents was an experience we will never forget. The archives were founded in 1378 and are presently located in central-northern Lisbon on the campus of the University of Lisbon. In 2009, the archives were renamed the **Instituto dos Arquivos Nacionais**.

How to get there

The Torre do Tombo address is Alameda da Universidade, 1649-010 Lisboa. We took an Uber only because we had an early appointment at the archives. But there are several buses that go to the University (Universidade de Lisboa) and the archives. You can also use the metro.
The website for the Archives has all the information for requesting a visit and how to get there:
https://antt.dglab.gov.pt/

The documents we saw detailed the questioning and trials of the accused Judaisers.
We were told that each document contained all sorts of "heretical" items: texts of Hebrew prayers, dish recipes, locations of hidden

Right: The Entrance to the National Archives, Torre do Tombo.

Jewish cemeteries, correspondence with Jews abroad, and mentioning of forbidden books or strange customs and rituals.

Documents from the Inquisition archives.

This badly damaged document is being prepared for conservation.

The author with the archives conservator, Sonia Domingos, study the Inquisition documents.

Every case was a story of human suffering. These pages, neatly written in a language we could not read, were true testimonies speaking of the tragedy of the Jewish people. The documents that Sonia shared with us came from Évora, the town where the Portuguese Inquisition was first established.

Why Almost No Traces of the Past Jewish Presence Can Be Found in Lisbon Today

Was that willful ignorance? Intentional forgetfulness? Or – something else?

Actually, all of the above. Of course, both ignorance and forgetfulness were prompted by the Edict of Expulsion of the Jews from Portugal immediately followed by the forced conversion of the entire Portuguese Jewish community. And then, the persecution by the Inquisition played a big role.

Another factor that falls in the category of "something else" was a devastating sequence of events that destroyed not only the traces of Jewish life in Lisbon but also leveled most of the city. A triple disaster: an earthquake, tsunami, and fire, all happened one after another early in November of 1755.

The Infamous Earthquake of 1755 and Marquês de Pombal (1699-1782)

The earthquake of 1755 was felt throughout the Iberian Peninsula and North Africa. It occurred in the morning of the first of November, which happened to be the Feast of All Saints holiday. Most of Lisbon was destroyed, and about 60,000 to 70,000 people were killed in Lisbon alone.

Marquês de Pombal (Marquise of Pombal).

He was the Secretary of the State of Internal Affairs of the Kingdom (similar to the Prime Minister today) in the government of King José I (1714-1777, ruled 1750-1777). Because the king was not interested in governing, Marquês de Pombal was a de facto leader of Portugal. He was a gifted and ambitious promoter of the democratic ideals of the Enlightenment. Pombal was praised as a great reformer and organizer but was also hated and feared for his ruthless tactics.

He worked against the Church's boundless power and repression, expelled the Jesuits to free the educational system from their domination, and broke off relations with the Pope. But even Pombal could not abolish the Inquisition. However, he managed to transform this institution of horror by bringing it under the state authority. In addition, Pombal also ended black slavery in Portugal. In the area of the economy, Pombal modernized Portuguese industry and commerce.

After the earthquake and tsunami destroyed Lisbon, within a month, Pombal began major rebuilding in much of today's historic center of the capital city. He came up with a grid plan for the world's first earthquake-proof buildings. In 1777, the king died, and Pombal, hated by many of his rivals, was dismissed and banished to his country estate. He died there in 1782.

For the New Christians, who even after hundreds of years and many generations after the conversion, were still considered "New" to Christianity and therefore hated and persecuted, Pombal was a hero. He was able to end the persecution of Portuguese citizens of Jewish descent.

A curious historical anecdote survived till this day: The Chief Inquisitor asked King José I to approve a new law that would require every New Christian to wear a yellow hat in public. If you think about it, by the time of the Inquisitor's proposal, these "New" Christians had been living as Christians for almost three hundred years.

Marquês de Pombal, who angrily objected to this medieval monstrosity of a proposal, came to court with three yellow hats. When the king asked who was supposed to wear those hats, Pombal responded: "One for me, one for you, and one for the Chief Inquisitor." The proposal was denied. However, the Inquisition was not abolished in Portugal until 1821.

"Meeting" Marquês de Pombal in Lisbon

When you are in the Commerce Square or Praça de Comércio, take a closer look at the majestic **Rua Augusta Arch.** It was built to commemorate Lisbon's quick recovery that followed the disastrous earthquake of 1755.

Praça de Comércio.

Rua Agusta Arch. Praça de Comércio.

In the photo on the bottom of the previous page, notice the two great personalities of Portuguese history: Pombal is on the right. Vasco da Gama is on the left.

In the middle of Praça de Comércio stands a monument to King José I. The king is on the horse. But Pombal is there too: he is in the medallion.

Left: King José I monument on Praça de Comércio.

Lisbon also has a monument dedicated to Pombal alone. **Praça do Marquês de Pombal** (the Marquis of Pombal Square) is located at the end of **Avenida da Liberdade** next to the park called **Parque Eduardo VII** in the quarter of Santo António.

Left: Praça do Marquês de Pombal.

Lisbon Museums through the Lens of a Jewish History Explorer

Arpad Szenes-Vieira da Silva Foundation

Look for paintings by Arpad Szenes, a famous Portuguese artist of Jewish origin. The museum is named after his wife Maria Helena Vieira da Silva who was also an artist.

You will find the museum in the Jardim das Amoreiras gardens, close to Aqueduto das Águas Livres (the aqueduct).
Address: Praça das Amoreiras, 56/58.
Website: https://fasvs.pt/

City Museum (Museu da Cidade)

Ask about the collection of engravings depicting the *autos-da-fé*.
Address: Campo Grande 245.
Website: https://www.museudelisboa.pt/pt

National Museum of Archeology (Museu Arqueológico do Carmo)

Observe the tombstones with Hebrew inscriptions.
Address: Largo do Carmo.
Website: https://www.museuarqueologicodocarmo.pt/

National Museum of Antique Art (Museu Nacional d'Arte Antigua)

Look for Painéis de São Vicente de Fora (the Saint Vincent Panels). There you find a Jewish man carrying a book in Hebrew. A truly unmissable work of art! The panels are attributed to Nuno Goncalves (15th century).
Address: Rua das Janelas Verdes.
Website: http://www.museudearteantiga.pt/

National Tiles Museum (Museu Nacional do Azulejo)

This museum contains an amazing collection of *Azulejo* tiles. Ask where to find the panel depicting Lisbon before the earthquake of 1755.

And do not miss the panels depicting scenes from the Old Testament: Abraham sacrificing Isaac and Pharaoh's daughter finding Moses in the basket.
Address: Rua Me. Deus, 4.
Website: http://www.museudoazulejo.pt/

Naval or Maritime Museum (Museu de Marinha)

As described in our Belém section, among other objects in the museum's extensive collection, you will find the navigational instruments developed by Jewish scientists.
Address: Praça do Império, Belém.
Website: https://ccm.marinha.pt/pt/museu

The Rebirth of the Jewish Community in Lisbon

The Long Process of Judaism Legalization

Since the times of Marquês de Pombal, Portuguese society had a strong anti-clerical sentiment. The Inquisition was abolished in 1821, and all religious orders were banned. As a result, the Church lost the majority of its properties.

In 1910, the Portuguese First Republic was established, the separation of Church and State was instituted, and education was secularized.

In the early 1930s, with the *Estado Novo* or "new state" under the totalitarian dictatorship of Antonio Salazar, the Church experienced a revival and became a strong force in Portugal once again. Anti-Semitism was encouraged and raised its ugly head.

As a result of the Carnation Revolution (1974) and the new Portuguese Constitution (1976), the separation of Church and State became official again. Although the Catholic faith remained very important for many Portuguese people, persons of other religions were allowed to openly practice their beliefs.

According to the JNS (*Jewish News Syndicate*), today, Portugal is home to approximately 6,000 Jews with the majority living in Lisbon and Porto. Each of these cities counts about 500 formally registered member families.

To find the **Great Synagogue of Lisbon,** go to Rua Alexandre Herculano and look for # 59.
Website: https://cilisboa.org/.
For visits: https://cilisboa.org/visitantes/. Inquire and register at visits@cilisboa.org

Lisbon Shaare Tikvah Synagogue, 1904

Inaugurated in 1904, Lisbon Synagogue became the first post-Expulsion synagogue in the Iberian Peninsula. The name "Shaare Tikvah" means the "Gate of Hope." The synagogue was designed by the famous architect of the time, Miguel Ventura Terra.

At the beginning of the 20th century, the synagogue building had to be located inside a walled yard. If a religious temple was not Catholic, it was still forbidden for the building to face the main road. Official legalization of the Jewish community was also impossible to obtain at that time.
So, the Jews of Lisbon formed

Right: Lisbon Synagogue.

various charities, either in the form of autonomous associations or as private foundations. Often run by women, these entities played a very important role in the life of the Portuguese Jewish community.

After an almost half-a-century effort, the small Jewish community of Lisbon bought land for the construction of their synagogue.

Lisbon Synagogue, view from the street Rua Alexandre Herculano.

Synagogue's interior.

Synagogue's interior.

The first stone was laid in 1902, and the building was inaugurated in 1904. The interior boasts a beautiful neo-oriental decor, and the synagogue is laid out according to the traditional plan of Ashkenazi synagogues.

At the time of the synagogue construction and inauguration, most members of Lisbon's Jewish community were Sephardic Jews, originally from either Gibraltar or North Africa. Others were either Russian or Polish Ashkenazi Jews escaping violent pogroms in their home countries.

Lisbon also has the only reform synagogue in Portugal called **Ohel Jacob** founded by Polish immigrants in 1930. Address: Rua Filipe da Mata, 1600-070 Lisboa.

Lisbon during World War II

Do you remember the last scene in the iconic movie "Casablanca" (1943)? Ingrid Bergman and Humphrey Bogard were saying their famous "goodbyes" while standing by the airplane that was getting ready to fly to… Lisbon. The capital city of neutral Portugal became a "promised land" for thousands of refugees from Nazism. If they were lucky to obtain a transit visa, it was Portugal, from where they could escape Fascist Europe and get to the United States or Latin America.

A Museum in the coastal town of Estoril is dedicated to the exiles seeking a safe haven in Portugal during the war. It was inaugurated by the President of Portugal in 2017.

One heroic person was instrumental in issuing transit visas to thousands of European Jews and other refugees. His name was **Aristides de Sousa Mendes** (1885-1954). He was a Portuguese consul-general in Bordeaux located in the Southwest of France. Defying Salazar's orders, Sousa Mendes kept issuing visas to thousands of desperate refugees. (You will read more about Sousa Mendes in our upcoming Guide to Central Portugal and its chapter on Cabanas.)

In addition to numerous Jewish refugees using transit visas to pass through Portugal, there were also royal families, politicians, famous artists, movie directors, writers (like Heinrich Mann or Antoine de Saint-Exupéry), and secret agents.

Lisbon as a Nest of Spies and Josephine Baker (1906-1975)

Lisbon during the Second World War became a true nest of spies. Lisbon and Estoril were important centers of European espionage and counter-espionage. Agents came from both sides, the Third Reich and the Allies. They congregated in casinos, bars, restaurants, and hotel lobbies in Lisbon, Estoril, and Cascais.

Hotel Avenida Palace (circa 1900) – the oldest hotel in Lisbon.

Left: The hotel's elegant bar was popular with World War II spies.

This twentieth-century Babylon consisted of American, British, French, German, and Italian intelligence officers mixed with Jewish refugees, members of exiled royal families, former bankers, and prominent artists and writers. Sometimes, one famous personality immediately recognized and admired by all would show up: **Josephine Baker.**

Baker, an African-American dancer, singer, and actress, was born in St. Louis, Missouri in 1906. She moved to France when she was not even twenty years old. In a few years, Baker became the toast of Paris as a much-venerated performer and a Jazz Age symbol. In 1927, at twenty-one, she starred in a popular movie *Siren of the Tropics*, the first woman of color cast in a leading role.

In 1939, even before Paris was occupied by the Nazis, Baker began working for the French Resistance and the French counter-intelligence. To exchange information with the Allies agents, she often traveled to Lisbon and secretly met with them at the British Embassy. You can come to number 33 on Rua de São Bernardo to see the building of the **British Embassy in Lisbon** where Baker's secret meetings took place.

"Her stardom was her cloak," wrote Damien Lewis in his book *Agent Josephine: American Beauty, French Hero, and British Spy* (Public Affairs, 2022). Even German soldiers seeing Baker on a railway platform would rush to her eager to catch her famous smile or get an autograph. After the war, Josephine Baker was awarded numerous medals: The French Committee of National Liberation awarded her the Resistance Medal. The French military gave Baker the *Croix de Guerre*. She was named a *Chevalier de la Légion d'honneur* (Knight of Legion of Honor) by Charles de Gaulle.

In November 2021, France bestowed the highest honor upon Josephine Baker as a symbol of gratitude for her life service: A decision was made to have her remains interred in a tomb at the Pantheon.

Not many know that Josephine was buried next to her husband in the Monaco Cemetery. She wanted to be buried there also because that was the country of her closest friend, Grace Kelly, the Princess of Monaco.

So, at the request of her family, Josephine Baker was not interred at the Pantheon physically, but instead, it was done symbolically. A Cenotaph with her name was ceremonially placed in the Pantheon Crypt number 13.

There, this beloved African-American heroine of France symbolically lies next to Voltaire, Jean-Jacques Rousseau, Victor Hugo, and Émile Zola. The day when Baker's Cenotaph was installed at the Pantheon, Prince Albert II of Monaco, son of Princess Grace, paid homage to Josephine at her grave in the Monaco Cemetery.

Jewish Community of Lisbon during the Second World War and Today

With the rise of Nazism all over Europe, violent persecution of the Jews, and the neutrality of Portugal, the small Jewish community of Lisbon had to undergo rapid changes in its size, the national origin of its members, and its goals and actions. In the 1930s, the first Ashkenazi Jews began to arrive in Portugal. When the war began, tens of thousands of Jewish refugees, transit visa holders, were pouring into the country.

Lisbon's Jewish community rose to the great challenge of supporting these refugees. First, they organized the "Portuguese Commission for Assistance to Jewish Refugees in Portugal" (COMASSIS), and soon after, formed the Refugee Support Section within the Lisbon community. Largely assisted by the funds coming from the American Joint Distribution Committee (the Joint) and other international Jewish charities, Lisbon Jews organized and maintained the Economic Kitchen and Israeli Hospital, meeting refugees' needs from food and clothing to medical care.

In recent years, a few milestone events prompted an increase in the number of Jews from different parts of the world arriving in Portugal: the political opening of the country after the Carnation Revolution in 1974, the entry of Portugal into the European Union in 1985, and the signing of the Organic Law (or Law of Return) in 2013. This law granted Portuguese citizenship to some descendants of Sephardic Jews expelled from the country in the 15th century. These events changed the makeup of the Jewish community of Lisbon and of the entire country.

At the present, there is no Jewish museum in Lisbon. However, this omission is about to be fixed soon.

The Jewish Museum is Coming to Lisbon!

Named Tikvá Museu Judaico Lisboa (*Tikva* means "hope" in Hebrew), the future museum is dedicated to the Jewish history of Portugal and, of course, of Lisbon. It will be built in Belém along the waterfront and close to the historic Belém Tower. The museum was designed by the world-famous architect Daniel Libeskind, whose architecture is highly symbolic and is meant to tell a story.

If you happened to see or were lucky to visit some of Libeskind's other museums, you are already familiar with his conceptual approach to architectural design. For example, his Contemporary Jewish Museum in San Francisco is shaped to spell *La Chaim* meaning "to life". The Jewish Museum in Copenhagen is shaped like the Hebrew word *Mitzvah*, which means "a good deed". The word reminds us of the heroic role Danish people played in saving practically the entire Jewish community of their country during the Holocaust. Likewise, in Lisbon, the upcoming Jewish museum will be shaped like the Hebrew word *Tikva*.

The Lisbon Jewish museum project has two main partners: the City Hall of Lisbon and a non-profit organization Association Haggadah, where *Haggadah* is meant to reflect the narrative of the Exodus of Jews from Egypt, which is read during the celebration of the Passover holiday.

Lisbon's oldest neighborhood Alfama was originally chosen as the site for the museum. However, in 2019, Association Haggadah received a lease on a plot of land in the Belém district located west of Lisbon, that came with a license to build a museum. This 50-year renewable lease was issued by the municipality of Lisbon.

The next event was very important for the future museum's project. In October of 2022, the Portugal Ministry of Culture officially announced the country's recognition of the cultural importance of the Jewish museum that would be built in Lisbon.

The goal of creating a Jewish museum in Lisbon is to educate diverse audiences about Sephardic Jewish history, promote Portuguese Jewish life, and highlight the contribution of the Jewish community to the history of Lisbon and beyond.

As the museum's director, Dr. Esther Mucznik announced in her press release: "The museum will tell a unique story of almost two thousand years of longevity and plurality of cultures that give Portuguese Judaism a peculiar and very rich character… It is this history and this memory that the museum…will make known to the national and foreign public."

You can find more information at the Tikvá Museu Judaico Lisboa website: https://mjlisboa.com/en/

SIDE TRIPS FROM LISBON

To deepen your understanding of Portugal, we suggest dedicating two or three days to exciting and history-packed side trips out of Lisbon to Sintra, Cabo da Roca, Mafra, Ericeira, Cascais, and Estoril.

Mafra and Ericeira could be combined with Cascais and Estoril into one long day trip, but this would require a car and meticulous planning.

Sintra

How to get there and when

Sintra is only about 28 kilometers from Lisbon, but we do not advise driving there, because traffic might be very heavy, and it is difficult finding a place to park in Sintra. Sintra is easily reached in 40 relaxed minutes by train from Rossio Station. If you have your Lisboa Card, then your train rides are covered and a part of your entrance tickets as well.

When planning your day in Sintra, remember that this World Heritage city is the most popular destination for millions of Lisbon visitors. Especially on Mondays, when almost all museums in Lisbon are closed, many visitors of the capital are heading to Sintra. So, it is a good idea to arrive in Sintra early in the morning by the time the main attractions begin to open. Taking an early train is also essential for beating the crowd.

If you are in Portugal during the "shoulder season" (spring and fall) and plan to start your visit with, for example, Pena Palace, be there when it opens at 9:30 AM. Don't forget to show your Lisboa Card at the box office to buy discounted tickets to the three key attractions: Pena Palace, Moorish Castle, and National Palace.

However, if you are traveling during the high season (June through September) we would suggest buying your single tickets online at least a few days in advance at https://www.parquesdesintra.pt/pt/

One more suggestion: upon exiting the train station in Sintra, look for bus number 434 and buy the all-day-ride ticket. This bus stops at all attractions, so you will have an easy way to get around.

Jewish Sintra

Historians think that there was a small pre-expulsion, pre-forced conversion Jewish community in Sintra. The first reference to the Jewish quarter of Sintra dates back to the 12th century. A few documents confirm the uneasy relationship between the small Jewish community and their Christian neighbors. For example, in the 15th century, King Afonso V received complaints from Sintra Christians that the Jews were extending their trade beyond their quarter into the city proper. The king decreed that Jews could only use the gateway to the Jewish quarter as a place of trade, and should not conduct their business beyond it.

The only trace of the long-gone Jewish presence you will be able to find is the name of a tiny street **Beco Judiaria** in the Sintra historical center.

Therefore, your day in Sintra will be dedicated to exploring its unique enchantments: phantasmagorical Pena Palace, dreamy ruins of the Moorish Castle, and the treasure trove of Portuguese history, National Palace.

Pena Palace

If you ever visited Neuschwanstein Castle in Schwangau, Bavaria, Germany, built by King Ludwig II (nicknamed "Mad Ludwig"), you might think that Ludwig's Castle and Pena Palace are close relatives. And indeed they are! "Mad Ludwig" of Bavaria and the Portuguese romantic prince Ferdinand were cousins. It is hard to say who influenced whom. King Ludwig built his castle in 1869, but Prince Ferdinand's Pena Palace was completed almost twelve years earlier, in 1854. Nevertheless, we had a strange feeling that these two flamboyant creations were in a constant dialogue, exchanging ideas.

View of the Pena Palace from the patio.

Pena Palace, now a World Heritage Site, seems to combine a strange mixture of Portuguese and German architectural influences with lots of Arabic minarets and Manueline-style decorations. We had great fun exploring architectural and decorative details both inside and outside the palace.

A decorative detail.

National Palace

This oldest existing palace in Portugal is a real treasure trove of history. The original structure was built on this

View of the National Palace from the Moorish Castle.

site during the Moorish period. But what you visit today dates back to the early 15th century, the time of King João I, the father of Henry the Navigator and husband to Philippa of Lancaster. Numerous Manueline-style decorative details were added later, during the rule of King Manuel I of Portugal.

A pair of unique chimneys of the National Palace as seen from the central patio.

Royal families occupied this palace for 500 years until the October Revolution of 1910 that abolished monarchy in the country. Notice the strange cone-shaped chimneys. Their design made sure that the smoke from the kitchens would not penetrate the rest of the building.

Enjoy touring one room after another, all the while following historical anecdotes that fill the atmosphere of every room in this unique palace. Refresh your knowledge of Portuguese history in advance: you will not find many explanatory signs inside!

We have a few of our favorites in this remarkable palace where every room reflects the rich country's history. The **Swan Room** is an impressive Gothic banquet hall. But for us, it also served as a demonstration of a father's love. When in 1430, King João's daughter Isabel married Philip the Good, Duke of Burgundy, the king missed her so much that he had this room dedicated to her. Look up: the ceiling is filled with images of Isabella's favorite bird, the swan.

Our other favorite is the **Magpie Room**. Again, look up at the ceiling. It is all painted with the symbol of gossip: a multitude of magpie birds.

This is how João I wanted to show his wife, Philippa of Lancaster, that this court is a huge nest of "magpies."

Painted ceiling in the Magpie Room.

He was saying to his dear wife not to pay any attention to numerous rumors about his love affairs! Each of these birds proclaims King's motto. Translated from Latin, it means "For good." No matter what the king was doing and with whom – it was all "For good."

If you are interested in Masonic philosophy and have time left after visiting the Moorish castle and two palaces, you might want to stop by **Quinta da Regaleira** castle and walk through its beautiful gardens infused with mystical and Masonic symbolism.

Moorish Castle

Moors built this castle over one thousand years ago and occupied it through 1147 when Afonso Henriques took it. You can get there by taking the bus number 434. In the 19th century, King Ferdinand incorporated the ruins into an imaginary medieval garden.

Cabo da Roca

If you want to take a selfie picture standing at the westernmost point of Portugal, go to Cabo da Roca.

How to get there
Unless you are driving there, the easiest way to Cabo da Roca from Sintra, would be to hire a taxi.

Right: Cabo da Roca. The author, shivering in the wind, stands at the westernmost point of the entire Eurasian landmass!

However, be warned: during any season and most of the time, this site will be filled with tourists. But it is an exciting destination nevertheless. You will find yourself at the westernmost point of not only mainland Portugal but also of continental Europe.

You might also want to accompany your Instagram photo with a famous quote from a 16th-century Portuguese poet Luís de Camões: "Where the land ends and the sea begins."

Mafra

How to get there
Mafra is about 40 km to the northwest of Lisbon via A8. On the day of our trip to Mafra, we rented a car at the Lisbon airport and pulled into a parking lot near Mafra's famous palace after driving for less than an hour. This paid parking is located to the left of the palace.

The Royal Palace in Mafra. Photo courtesy of Directorate-General for Cultural Heritage, Photographic Documentation Archive, Mafra National Palace.

The royal palace in Mafra is one of the largest in Europe and is considered the most important example of Baroque architecture in Portugal. According to the Mafra National

Palace's brochure, this massive building covers an area of over four hectares (almost ten acres) and boasts close to 5,000 doors and windows, 1200 rooms, 156 stairways, and 29 inner courtyards. The palace construction began in 1717 and was completed in 1755. How could anyone, even a king, afford this? The answer is very simple: gold from Brazil.

Approaching the palace, you encounter a statue of King João V (1689-1750, ruled 1706-1750) who built it as a "Thank you, God" for the birth of his first child. The king meant to build a convent (his first, long-awaited child was a girl), but the intended structure for nuns was decorated like a royal residence.

Right: Statue of King João V.

Even if you plan to quickly visit all the splendid rooms in this national monument, do try to slow down and stop by the church or the Basilica of the Royal Palace and observe the six pipe organs there, which were designed as a set and could be played simultaneously.

We particularly wanted to see two rooms within the palace: the **Library** and the **Hall of Portuguese Heroes**.

Mafra Library, priceless books, and the bats that "guard" them

This great library contains over 36,000 volumes that cover a multitude of disciplines, such as alchemy, various sciences, and theology, to name just a few. The collection also includes its famous treasure: illuminated Books of Hours dating back to the 15th century.

The library is designed in a form of a cross with amazing polychromic marble floors and rocaille shelves. Rocaille is the 18th-century decorative style, usually encountered in grottoes, fountains, and furniture.

Right: The "forbidden" books in the library of Mafra Palace. Photo courtesy of Directorate-General for Cultural Heritage, Photographic Documentation Archive, Mafra National Palace.

We could not take our eyes off the library shelves. Their elegant curves and counter-curves seemed to be dancing: smoothly rising and falling. The second-floor shelves contain the "forbidden" books that were banned by the Inquisition. However, the monks, who were in charge of the library, defied the orders to destroy these books and hid the precious volumes instead.

We also found out that the library "employed" bats to "guard" the fragile ancient manuscripts from bookworms and moths. This is how it works, we were explained. In the evening, the library staff opens the windows, and the bat army arrives in mass from the outside: swooping among the shelves and eating the insects that would otherwise destroy the books. Who could have thought of that? It is not known when this defensive "bat maneuver" was first deployed. We were told that this practice has been going on for centuries.

The Hall of Portuguese Heroes and the Secrets of its Frescos

If you have binoculars, bring them with you. When you enter the Hall of Portuguese Heroes, take a good look at the ceiling fresco. This hall was the main reason for us to come to Mafra Palace: to examine what we thought might (or might not) be historical truth. The Portuguese heroes painted on this ceiling are those who defined the Age of Discoveries and made Portugal the most powerful, wealthiest, and knowledgeable nation in Europe. According to what we learned from the staff, the ceiling was painted on the orders given by the king himself.

Only two images on this fresco have precise identification. Look at the first figure in the left upper corner that has "Infant Henrique de Portugal" written on the shield. That identifies Henry of Portugal, who we know in English as **Prince Henry the Navigator**.

On the right top of the fresco, notice a figure fighting a sea monster: Most historians think this image depicts **Vasco da Gama** (1460-1524). However, other historians think that it could be **Duarte Pacheco Pereira** (1460-

1533), an explorer and scientist. He possibly visited Brazil a few years prior to 1500, when Brazil was "officially" announced as the great discovery attributed to **Pedro Álvares Cabral**.

Mafra Palace. Hall of Portuguese Heroes. Fresco on the ceiling. Photo courtesy of Directorate-General for Cultural Heritage, Photographic Documentation Archive, Mafra National Palace.

Indeed, it is logical to expect that for this king, the place of utmost importance was Brazil (Pereira), and not India (Da Gama). After all, it was gold from Brazil that paid for the Royal Palace in Mafra. And the king should also have known that it was Pereira, not Cabral, who first explored and described the new land full of riches, like gold and "Brazilwood," hence the name of the new country.

However, **Pedro Cabral** is also not forgotten of course. It is believed that he is portrayed in the left bottom corner, pushed up to his fame by a winged figure.

Take a close look at the fourth figure (in chains), which, in addition to Prince Henry, is the only other person identified in this fresco. This is also the only figure that has an identification of that person's great services to Portugal. Two winged angels are holding a banner that proclaims in Latin: "A CASTILLA Y LEÓN NUEVO MUNDO DIO COLON." Which, if you use Google Translator, will bring you this: "To Castile and Leon a New World Gave Columbus."

Ask Google where Christopher Columbus was born. The answer will be in Genoa, Italy. And this was what we and many of our friends and readers learned in school.

And now ask yourself: If Columbus was an Italian, why is he in the Hall of Portuguese Heroes? Moreover, why would a Portuguese King glorify someone who worked for the biggest rivals of Portugal, King Ferdinand of Aragon and Queen Isabella of Castile, and discovered a New World for them?

Next, why was this figure in chains given such importance as to have identification, unlike other figures, except for Prince Henry? In addition, this Portuguese hero has something that even the Navigator does not: a description of what he did and for whom. He discovered a new world for Spain.

Before we proceed any further, I want to make a disclaimer:

The purpose of this section is not to proclaim an absolute truth and the only truth about Columbus's identity and the conspiracies and espionage that saturated the Age of Discoveries. My goal was to raise questions, not to provide unquestionable answers. I also wanted the readers of this book to fall in love with Portugal and its history, which keeps many secrets and could be read and looked upon through numerous lenses and from so many different angles, while uncovering unexpected surprises at every turn.

And now, let us pose a few intriguing questions:

Was it the Age of Discoveries or the age of carefully planned deceits and disclosures?
Who indeed was the person known to us as Christopher Columbus or Cristobal Colon? And why is he depicted in chains?

The last question about the chains is the easiest one, and it is a well-known and often repeated story. After Columbus's third voyage, while he was the governor of Hispaniola, he was indeed arrested and brought back to Spain in chains to stand trial before the king. What was he accused of?

As often happens in Portuguese history, there is no single answer. Was Columbus accused of taking severe actions against rebellious European settlers?
Or – of misappropriating the colony's money?
Or – of his cruel treatment of native people?

The answer depends on who tells this story and where you read it. But the following fact is documented: while King Ferdinand stripped Columbus of his governorship, he gave him his freedom and paid for the next voyage.

Who was this man we know as Christopher Columbus (1451-1506)?

As I learned while in Portugal, today, more and more historians and heritage guides alike believe that his real name was **Salvador Fernandes Zarco**, a man of Sephardic origin born in a little Portuguese town in Alentejo called Cuba. By the way, Columbus named the second Caribbean island that he discovered, "Cuba."

I would like now to address the question concerning Columbus's possible Judaism that I am asked frequently. A number of researchers and history writers state that the man we know as Columbus, but whose real name might have been Salvador Fernandes Zarco, was indeed of Sephardic origin.

But did he consider himself a Jew or a Crypto-Jew? Historians believe that in letters to his sons, Columbus often wrote B***H*** for *Baruch Hashem*, thus invoking the God of the Jews. In his will, Columbus left money to orphaned girls for their dowries, and that was a traditional *mitzvah* (a charity gift) for Jews. Some also speculate that Columbus delayed his departure for the New World so as not to coincide with *Tisha B'Av*, a Jewish holy day that annually commemorates the destruction of the First and Second Temples in Jerusalem, as well as numerous other calamities experienced by Jewish people over the centuries.

Next question: Was Columbus a commoner, a son of a Genovese wool weaver? Or, could he be a Portuguese aristocrat and a spy for the king?

And, here is the key question: Did Columbus REALLY think he was sailing to India in 1492?

What we can now assume with a large degree of certainty is that the Age of Discoveries was taking place in a world of complicated conspiracies and twisted political intrigues, just like in John Le Carre's spy novels!

What we do know for sure:

The key economic, commercial, and political interests of all European powers at that time were focused on India and India only. Why? The Ottoman sultans had allowed only two European city-states, Genoa and Venice, to import spices from the East and only through Islamic lands. So, whoever was the first to discover a sea route to India would be able to bypass that Ottoman embargo and be the first to pocket all the profits.

It has become common knowledge that Columbus appeared at the court of Spanish Royalty in Seville sometime during the 1480s with his proposal to reach India by sailing westwards. It is also often mentioned that Columbus explained to Ferdinand and Isabella that his proposal met no interest at the Portuguese court.

Three more questions to consider:

First, is it possible to even imagine a commoner, son of a Genoese weaver, being easily admitted at both, the Portuguese and the Spanish courts?

Second, why do we know close to nothing about Columbus prior to his appearance in Seville?

And finally, why did King João II fail to show any interest in Columbus's proposal when every European power dreamed of reaching India by sea?

The answer to the third question might (or might not) be very simple: Perhaps, Portuguese King João II already knew through his explorer-spy Pêro da Covilhã that it was possible to reach the real India by sea. (See the Age of Discoveries section about Pêro da Covilhã).

Additionally, perhaps the king also knew of the existence of "other Indies," which were not the "real" India, but instead a large continent and numerous islands that had no gold and no spices.

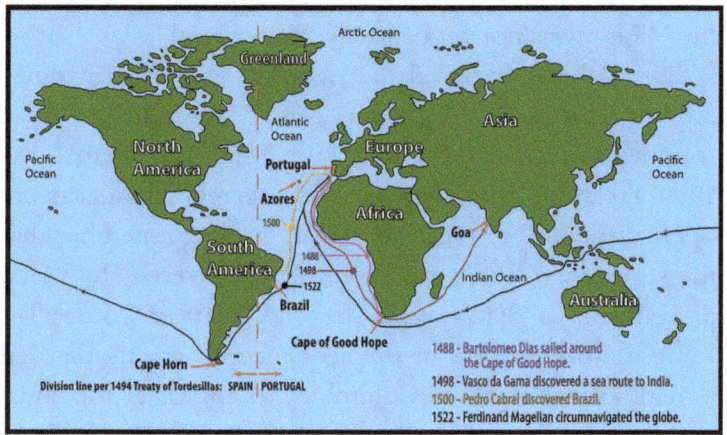

The vertical red line denotes a divider per the Treaty of Tordesillas signed by Spain and Portugal in 1494.

Take a second look at the map of the great Portuguese discoveries, which you have already seen. Pay special attention to the vertical red line that denotes a divider per the **Treaty of Tordesillas** signed by Spain and Portugal in 1494.

At the continuous insistence of Pope Alexander VI, hostile rivals Spain and Portugal agreed to meet in the Spanish city of Tordesillas to divide the already known and yet-to-be-discovered and colonized "New World."

The Portuguese stubbornly argued for the dividing meridian to be where you can see it on the map. The Spaniards finally agreed. If you look closely, you will notice that Spain received North America, part of South America, and numerous Caribbean islands, which they thought of as India. This indeed was that "New World" given to the Spaniards in 1492: "To Castile and Leon a New World Gave Columbus."

Portugal ended up with the richest part of the South American continent that would eventually become Brazil (in 1494, it was not yet officially "discovered").

Portugal also received the rights to explore sea routes around Africa. Bartolomeu (or Bartholomew) Diaz rounded the Cape of Good Hope six years before the 1494 Treaty, and Portugal kept it a secret. This discovery opened the way to reach the "real" India. Remember that the sea route to India was "officially discovered" by Vasco da Gama in 1498, four years after the Treaty of Tordesillas.

Let us briefly look at the sequence of events that led a man, known to us as Columbus, to appear at the court of Ferdinand and Isabella. In 1483, there was a plot to assassinate João II of Portugal. The plot was discovered, and the key conspirators were executed, including the queen's brother.

The rest of the plotters were exiled, and a number of them came to Spain, which most probably had a hand in planning the assassination. Some historians speculate that the persona of Cristobal Colon as one of the exiled plotters was invented in Portugal right around that time. His mission might have been to dupe the Spaniards into believing that he would discover the sea route to India for them. And thus, he would take Spain's attention away from what the Portuguese were really doing. In his letters, King João II often mentioned "our special friend in Seville."

Then, in 1488, Bartolomeu Diaz rounded the Cape of Good Hope. This event might have confirmed what the king most probably already knew: This was the sea route to reach India, which would be officially "discovered" by Da Gama ten years later, in 1498.

Of course, it is close to impossible to prove this hypothesis as absolute truth. But (there are always many "buts" in Portuguese history), why was Columbus not in a hurry to rush back to Spain after his first great voyage when he discovered the New World? Instead, he stopped in Portugal and spent about two weeks there meeting with the king and the queen before sailing to Spain.

If you would like to read more about the 15th-century espionage, conspiracies, Columbus's identity, and New World discoveries, I would like to recommend a few books on the subject. Here they are below:

Brown, R., and Barreto, M. *The Portuguese Columbus: Secret Agent of King John II*. Palgrave MacMillan, 1992.

Laranjeiro, P. *The Portuguese Who Discovered America: The Epic Voyage of Salvador Fernandes Zarco Better Known as Christopher Columbus*. Algarve History Association, 2008.

Santos, J.R. Codex 632: *The Secret of Christopher Columbus*. William Morrow & Company, 2009.

Following the Steps of the Refugees from the Nazis during WWII

A short drive from Mafra will bring you to a very different exploration trail: you will be retracing the steps of refugees from war-torn European countries, who found their safe haven in Portugal. Many were settled in little coastal towns of what is known as the Portuguese Riviera. The majority of these refugees were Jewish.

Ericeira

How to get there
It is only ten kilometers or a 12-15 minute drive to get from Mafra Palace to Ericeira. We were there at the end of March, and it was windy and cold. The streets and the beaches were empty, but we still enjoyed this beautiful seaside town. If you come to Ericeira during the summer season, you can explore its famous beaches, forty in number! You will also encounter crowds of people because Ericeira is known as the surfing capital of Europe.

If you are a summertime beach lover and your schedule allows, we recommend splitting your coastal explorations near Lisbon into two separate side trips: visit Mafra and Ericeira on the same day and then enjoy Cascais and Estoril on a different day. As for us, we covered Mafra and the three coastal cities in one day. But we arrived in the Portuguese Riviera when it was too cold to enjoy the beach!

For Jewish history seekers like us, Ericeira was one of the coastal towns, along with Cascais and Estoril, where the stateless Jewish refugees were resettled during the Second World War.

View of Ericeira Beach.

Cascais

How to get there

Cascais is only about 33 km from Lisbon via A5 or 38 km from Mafra via N9 and A16.

If you do not have a car, you can easily get there from Lisbon in 40 minutes by train departing from the Cais do Sodre train station. Your Lisboa Card will cover the cost. And since Cascais is the last stop, it is hard to miss it.

Cascais is an elegant and welcoming seafront resort town, especially enjoyable for many beach lovers during the summer months. When in the early 1900s, the queen chose Cascais as her summer vacation place, aristocracy followed, and they turned this small coastal village into the most fashionable spot to get away from Lisbon heat.

View of the Cascais harbor, marina, and citadel.

Cidadela de Cascais.

Palácio Seixas, Cascais.

Today, Cascais is loved by tourists from all over the world who come to Portugal in summer.

The Cascais Jewish Community was first documented when King Pedro I declared Cascais as a town in 1364.

Today, no traces of this long gone Jewish community can be found in Cascais. We only know from the Inquisition records that a number of Cascais Jews were accused of Judaizing and condemned.

Both Cascais and nearby Estoril, which is a town in the Municipality of Cascais, earned their place in modern Jewish history as a safe haven for many important Jewish personalities during the 1930s and 1940s. Among the refugees from the Nazi-occupied countries that came to Cascais and Estoril were Stephan Zweig, a renowned Austrian novelist and playwright; Franz Werfel, an Austrian-Bohemian novelist, playwright and poet; Peggy Guggenheim, a legendary American art collector; Max Ophüls, a famous German-French film director; and Leonid Hurwicz, a Polish-American genius mathematician, to name just a few.

Estoril

How to get from Cascais to Estoril
Estoril is a beautiful resort town situated next to Cascais. If you do not mind walking, you can get from the Cascais harbor to Estoril in about half an hour of the most delightful stroll along the seaside promenade. We learned that, though Estoril is a town in the municipality of Cascais, and both are beach resort towns, there is a big difference between the two.

Cascais is often mentioned as the most livable place in Portugal because of its high quality of life. The tiny Estoril, is famous for its luxurious hotels and one of the biggest working casinos in Europe. It is considered the most expensive place to live in the entire Iberian Peninsula.

Casino Estoril.

Built in the modernist style, Casino Estoril is also famous because the very first James Bond movie *Casino Royal* was filmed there.

During the Second World War, Casino Estoril and the Palace Hotel bars became places where spies from all sides congregated. Ian Fleming (1908-1964) found himself in neutral Portugal, including Estoril, during WWII. Later, the atmosphere of that nest of spies inspired him to write his famous James Bond novels.

Ian Fleming, James Bond, spies, Estoril, and an unexpected Jewish connection

The James Bond character was most probably based on Dusko Popov, a Serbian spy and British double agent, whose personality made a strong impression on Fleming, according to his literary critics.

Ian Fleming and the Spies' Network: Fleming worked as a personal assistant to none other than Rear Admiral John Godfrey, the Director of the Naval Intelligence. In May 1941, Godfrey took Fleming with him to make a short stop in Lisbon before going to Washington. While in Lisbon, they most likely visited a renowned bar in Lisbon's Avenida Palace Hotel, where intelligence agents from all over the world congregated during WWII.

For Admiral Godfrey, the main purpose of this trip to Washington D.C. was to establish intelligence cooperation between the U.K. and the U.S.A. And for that, London wanted Washington to create an intelligence agency similar to MI6. While Godfrey was in talks with Roosevelt, Fleming assisted in charting a document that outlined how the proposed new agency should be organized and operated. His draft was used to create the Office of Strategic Services, which later became the CIA.

When Geoffrey and Fleming returned to Portugal, Fleming was assigned to observe and analyze Dusko Popov's activities in Estoril. Both Fleming and Popov, along with a multitude of journalists and spies, stayed at the Palacio Hotel in Estoril and often bumped into each other in the casino and the bars.

Fleming's Jewish (and big financial business) connections: Ian Fleming came from a wealthy family connected with the banking house Robert Fleming & Co., which was founded by his grandfather. Ian's father was a Member of Parliament. Young Fleming was educated at the famous Eaton School and universities in Munich and Geneva.

Rich cosmopolitan socialite, Ian Fleming moved through several jobs including a brief employment at Reuters where he worked as an assistant-editor and journalist. Under pressure from his family, Ian Fleming went to work for a financial entity called Cull & Company, which was founded by a very successful stockbroker Gilbert Russell. This was how in the 1930s, the Russells entered Fleming's life, and Ian met a Jewish woman who was to play a very important role in it: Maud Russell.

Gilbert Russell, a well-connected aristocrat from the Dukes of Bedford family, was probably instrumental in Ian Fleming getting a job at the Naval Intelligence Division. And it was Gilbert Russell, who introduced Ian to his Jewish wife Maud, a society hostess and a renowned French art collector.

Maud came from a very rich London family of a Jewish father and a non-Jewish mother, but she and Gilbert always stressed her formidable German-Jewish identity. It is known that Maud tried very hard and used her connections and money to help her father's family to escape Nazi Germany. After the Kristallnacht, Maud flew to Cologne, Germany, to help her cousins.

When they met, Ian Fleming was only 23 years old and Maud Russell was 40, but they developed a very strong mutual attraction. Fleming became a regular guest at Mottisfont, Russell's beautiful estate in Hampshire. He often appeared at the glamorous parties Maud gave in her Knightsbridge home. These parties were attended by famous musicians, artists, collectors, poets, writers, and politicians. Among Maud's artistic acquaintances and friends were Henri Matisse, Rex Whistler, Boris Anrep, and famous photographer Cecil Beaton.

Maud's granddaughter, Emily Russell, who was an editor and publisher of Maud's dairies, was convinced that her grandmother and Ian Fleming had an affair, both before and during the war, and a deep friendship and attachment to each other throughout their lives. (See Russell, E. *A Constant Heart: The War Diaries of Maud Russell 1938-1945*, Dovecote Press, 2017).

Maud kept an envelope hidden within her personal papers with a black hair lock in it, marked as "I." Her husband Gilbert died of asthma in the early 1940s, but he did not have much of a presence in her diaries during his life. According to her granddaughter, Maud called Ian Fleming "the spy who saved me."

During the war years, thanks to Fleming, she was given a volunteer job at the Admiralty in the Naval Intelligence Division, and she treasured that opportunity to contribute to the war effort. When the war ended, so did her work and, probably, her affair with Fleming. In her diaries, Maud began mentioning Gilbert with a sense of grief and desolation. "I wish I could have died with G," her granddaughter quoted.

The Exiles Memorial Center and Museum or Espaço Memória dos Exílios

In 1999, the Cascais Municipal Council inaugurated the **Espaço Memória dos Exílios**, the Museum of Refugees or Exiles Memorial Center. This Center contains a rich collection of documents that preserve the memory of those famous and anonymous Jewish refugees who survived because the coastal cities of the Portuguese Riviera gave them an asylum from certain deportation and death.

Exiles Memorial Center, Estoril.

Symbolically, the Center is located on the upper floor of a modern-day post office. The reference is to the wartime

Estoril post office, where refugees gathered to receive news about their loved ones.

The Museum is located in the center of Estoril, in a building designed by the famous Portuguese modernist architect Adelino Nunes. In addition to the well-organized exhibit of archival documents, photographs, and personal items, there is also a specialized research library.

Banner on the Exiles Memorial Center.

Inside the Memorial Center.

Contact the Center in advance to check their working hours.

The website is: https://cultura.cascais.pt/list/museu/espaco-memoria-dos-exilios
The address: Avenue Marginal 7152 B-2765-192 Estoril
Tel. 352-214-815-930. Email: eme@cm-cascais.pt

The Parting Words

This concludes our "Shaland's Lisbon: An Illustrated Guide to Jewish History and Sites in and around Lisbon." Both the author and the illustrator/photographer hope you found it informative and useful. Please let us know your thoughts and suggestions. Send your email to alex.shaland.gtabooks@gmail.com.

We will also highly appreciate it if you review our book on Amazon.

So, what is next? Stay tuned for the following guides from the Portuguese series dedicated to Evora, Central Portugal, and the North of Portugal. The series's final book will focus on the Azores and Madeira archipelagos.

If you sign up for Irene Shaland's Newsletter at https://globaltravelauthors.com/, you will be the first to know when each of these books becomes available.

Happy reading and happy travels!
Irene and Alex Shaland

Support for the creation of this book was provided by the following individuals, organizations, and companies:

visitPortugal
Visitportugal is the official website of the national board of tourism in Portugal www.visitportugal.com/en

Center of Portugal Tourism
Center of Portugal Tourism is the official organization promoting and organizing tourism to the central part of Portugal as a spiritual and cultural center of the country. https://www.centerofportugal.com/

Alegretur
Alegretur is a tour operator specializing in religious and historical tourism. https://alegretur.com

About the Author

For Irene Shaland, globe-trotting is a passion and a way of life. She sees travel as a process of personal growth and an opportunity to share her knowledge and experiences with her readers who are also enthusiastic about history, arts, and legends from the four corners of the earth. Irene and her husband Alex have visited close to 90 countries and enchanted audiences with their books, magazine articles, lectures, and photography exhibits based on their travels.

Irene Shaland is an internationally published art and travel writer, Jewish historian, and educator. In her research, publications, and lectures she focuses on the rich tapestry of global Jewish experiences, culture, and heritage. Her third book *The Dao of Being Jewish and Other Stories* was released in 2016. Irene's new series dedicated specifically to Jewish history travel around the world was launched in September 2021 with the publication of *Shaland's Jewish Travel Guide to Malta and Corsica: A Trusted Travel Companion for the Jewish History Explorer.*

Irene's close to thirty articles were published in the U.S., Canada, U.K., France, South Africa, and Israel. A sought-after presenter, Irene lectures extensively nationally and internationally at conferences, research centers, synagogues, art galleries, art societies, Jewish Federations, and other Jewish institutions. She is the President of the GTA Books publishing company and a founding member of the Global Travel Authors Group.

About the Photographer

Alex Shaland is the author of *Suburbanites on Safari* (2019), and a popular series of children's books *Jackie the Penguin Goes on Safari* (2022) and *Jackie the Penguin Goes to Madagascar* (2023). Alex is also an internationally published photographer. His photographs appeared in various journals and other media in the U.S., Canada, France, Kenya, South Korea, and the U.K.

> Website: https://globaltravelauthors.com
> Twitter: @ShalandGTA
> Facebook:
> https://www.facebook.com/GlobalTravelAuthors

www.ingramcontent.com/pod-product-compliance
Lightning Source LLC
LaVergne TN
LVHW020414070526
838199LV00054B/3609